THE NICE THING ABOUT STRANGERS

The Nice Thing About Strangers

Non-Fiction Short Stories: Travel, Oldsters, Love, and Compassion

Paige M.J. Erickson

pmj.NTAS Press

Published by pmj.NTAS Press

ISBN: 978-0-692-59078-2

Typesetting services by BOOKOW.COM

Contents

PREFACE

Welcome to this collection of very short non-fiction stories. Whether traveling or at home, I seem to find only the beautiful, vulnerable, breathtakingly human things one can discover in strangers.

I'm a Colorado native and the fourth of five children. Always bookish, sometimes shy to a fault, going abroad was a way to compel myself into bravery. Writing in a notebook is how I navigate the world. (In fact, I'm writing now at baggage claim in Ataturk Airport, Istanbul and making a lot of people nervous.) I went to Austria for the novelists and the pastries, to Croatia for the sea and the mopeds, and to Turkey for the language and the salesmen.

I realized I was crafting something in my copious coping notes. I started my blog The Nice Thing about Strangers in 2011. It took me about two years before I would allow myself a role in the stories. At first, I just wanted to observe others. Then the overall practice of posting took away some of my shyness, and motivated me to share my role in the scenes.

By giving myself blog deadlines, I had to keep my eyes open for material. Nice things appeared to me in variety and abundance. I've learned more about compassion. I've learned a new patience–so many stories appear when I am waiting for airplanes, standing in public transportation, or heading elsewhere. Things that frustrated me have become opportunities to re-direct, to laugh, to look someone in the eye. I kept forcing myself to places where I would be a stranger, but I still found kindness and reasons to stay optimistic.

In compiling the stories from the blog, and adding a few new tales, I wanted a neat division of chapters, but this hasn't exactly worked according to plan. Turkey has monopolized my dreams and my notebooks for the past few years. So we'll spend more time in Turkey than anywhere else.

I hope you'll enjoy the stories. My wish has stayed the same in my four years of blogging. I write with the hope that you will also notice the strangers who surround you, and that you may observe them with a merciful view.

You may check out more stories, photos, and content here:

http://www.TheNiceThingAboutStrangers.com

Stories from Turkey

Weight Weight...Don't Tell Me

Waiting for a three a.m. flight after their vacation, the couple decides to weigh themselves on an airport baggage scale. She giggles before stepping up on the square silver platform. Her husband takes the coat she removed, a puffy beige one with fur lining, but she remains in her black boots with heavy gold buckles. She stares at the changing digits and laughs boldly when the numbers settle on her score. Winking at her husband, she accepts his hand as he helps her down.

Then he takes a turn himself. She peers over his shoulder. When his weight displays they both grow still, look away from each other as he climbs down. He assists her in putting on the coat, taking a glance at his stomach when she turns her back.

This bold misuse of the baggage scale begins a trend. It sets off a curiosity among the bored travelers resting in the airport before early morning connections. A man in a tracksuit gives it a try. Then a mother and child, two women in headscarves, various members of the airport cleaning crew.

Finally, an extremely old man wants to give it a shot. As the man wobbles unsteadily on the scale, a terminal full of strangers sit up and involuntarily reach out their arms—as though they can steady him from across the divide.

—Istanbul

Macho Maço Man

He struts wide, pacing to both sides of the sidewalk as he walks. He thrusts his arms out, adjusting his button-up shirt on his frame, propelling himself forward with a masculine directive. He clutches his cell phone in one hand, awaiting the decisions that might require his approval. He crosses at the crosswalk without fear or anxiety. He greets a policeman with a solid nod of his head.

His cell phone rings. It plays not a song or a light chirping, not the traditional Turkish tunes selected by more sentimental creatures, but a true telephone ring—the sort to which a real man would respond. He lifts the phone without checking the screen to identify the caller. He takes charge. "Efendim?" He answers.

Almost immediately, he slows his pace, his shoulders hunch down, his frame softens, he grows smaller, meek. He steps to an alley to clear the busy path for others. His voice warms: "Annem?" His mother is on the other end; she interrupts his command of the world, but he is pleased. His mother dials his number and the man becomes her boy.

—Izmir

Seaside Sobbing

At the park, the family waits for their turn on a swing. The huge contraption has two benches that face each other so the family can all sit together—knees to knees—and sway back and forth. Mom and daughter take the side facing the sea. Dad holds the toddler son. The son gapes from under a blue hat, horrified by the structure now caging his mother, and not in the mood to join her.

Dad climbs on anyway as the child screams and cries. Dad tucks the squirming boy under one arm and takes a picture of his wife and daughter with his free hand. Then he passes their camera. The child sobs on, facing his mother as she mops up his tears, but the father seems to think his son is only warming up to the experience. Dad wants pictures with the coast in the background. The mother seems to object, but yields since her husband laughs, saying "eeee, eeee," delighted to be with his family on such a lovely evening. So she snaps photos of her sobbing son and his beaming father, with the sea shining behind them, so they can always remember their holidays.

—Kuşadası

Afraid of the Dentist

The waiting room of the dental hospital is at the center of four hallways, lined with tons of small rooms where procedures are taking place. It feels a bit like The Price is Right. There are televisions everywhere, names flashing on the screens, bells chiming, and people hustling when hailed. A woman in a headscarf and a long jacket is scowling at me. My friend mutters, "Oh, she doesn't like you." I've been laughing and talking with this friend, writing in my notebook, and wearing a sleeveless dress. I assume any of these transgressions could explain her glare in my direction. It's 75 degrees in November, and I can't bear to wear long-sleeves. I admire her fortitude at being able to cover up, and I try to blink kindly in her direction. She just keeps casting a grumpy stare in return.

I head to the restroom to wash my hands and she follows. She approaches the sink next to mine, leaning toward the mirror to inspect her mouth. She laments to me in Turkish about her woes, but I can only understand about thirty percent of what she's said. I say, "Geçmiş olsun," which means "May it be in the past," and which is a typical condolence to offer someone sick or in pain. She turns and shows me her bleeding gums and broken teeth and laments that she looks ugly, seeking more commiseration than the standard phrase.

The question I want to ask is if the dentists will be able to repair her smile. What I cobble together from the words I know is: "Dentist can make a construction? Possible?" She gives me a reasonably confused look. I explain in Turkish, "I'm so sorry. I'm a foreigner. I am learning Turkish, but–," and she lights up. "Oh my girl," she sighs, "My daughter, thank you." Now perhaps my sleevelessness makes sense, as her prior scowl certainly does. So we return to the waiting room as friends, smiling over those with mouths full of gauze and minds full of dread.

—Istanbul

Linger, Loiter

The pair will meet in the Kültürpark. This space is filled with palm trees and idle folks napping on benches, completing Sudoku on benches, staring into space on benches. A grandfather takes his small grandson around the perimeter on a whisper-silent moped. A stray cat pauses in the greenery to let a stray dog pass.

The pair spots each other. He rises from his place beneath a tree to greet her. He stands as she passes a bored security guard manning the gate, as she waits for slow joggers to clear her path to him. She wears an orange scoop-neck shirt and her hair wound up in a bun. They hug. They hug with their torsos together, but then lean back from each other while still holding on—no kissing, no long stares—so it is hard to gauge their relationship. They pat each other. He on her lower back five times with both hands, she on his shoulders four times, then he on her back again four times.

They sit and chat as the heat of the day lifts, as a cool breeze finds its way from the water. They sit with a distance between them, but still close. They reveal their pleasure at being in the same place, but not much more. They rest their hands on their knees.

The officer watches them between scuffing his shoes on the cement and glancing at the gate he's supposed to be guarding. He stretches, twists at the waist, then looks back again at the two rather boring people under the tree, behaving themselves immensely.

—Izmir

Inspire Curiosity

Men who sell simit—a bagel-pretzel coated in toasted sesame seeds—are almost as ubiquitous in Istanbul as well-fed stray cats. Since I often took the same streets, I often passed the same simit salesman. We bonded by blinking at each other. Some days he was decked out in a houndstooth coat and beige fedora. On this day, he went sporty with a gray jacket and a navy Adidas cap.

As I approached, he gave me our blink of recognition. In Turkish, I asked if I could take his photo. My Istanbul days were dwindling, so I needed to pack my souvenirs. Though I knew it well, the question came out: "Can I take *my* picture?" But he forgave me. "Of me?" Yes, yes, I reached apologetically for my camera and offered up my mother's smile.

A crowd of men on a bench nearby began to chatter among themselves like pigeons. I turned to see if there was anyone there worth capturing. They went quiet as my simit man got himself into a pose. We kept on in Turkish. "Should I wear my hat?

I grinned, "If you want."

He took the hat off. "Oh, but I'm not beautiful," he said smoothing his gray hair.

"You are, you are!" I insisted with a click.

I showed him the photo on the camera's screen, which he gave a furtive look before sending me on my way. He stepped toward his friends, trying to blend back into the crowd of men. Like schoolboys, they teased him as he chuckled to himself. I walked away beaming, causing a few strangers down the street to wonder why that woman over there should seem so pleased.

—Istanbul

Siblings and 'Staches

The youngest child of a huge family is drinking Ayran, a beverage made of yogurt and water, as far as I can tell. She is at a table packed with siblings, elbow to elbow, eating their lunch hurriedly at a sidewalk café in the early afternoon. The girl spills a few drops of her drink into her lap. Her eyes widen and she looks left to right like a character in a cartoon. When she notices that no one has noticed, she pats the spots in her lap, soaking them into her slacks, then wipes her hand on a napkin before another sip.

She wears a white mustache from her drink. Her slightly older brother is standing at the head of the table and gestures to her. She beams at him, raising the yogurt mustache in an upward turn. It seems he wants to tell her about her accessory without everyone at the table noticing, and they continue a helpless game of charades until she begins to shadow his movements. He holds a napkin to his mouth. She does as well. Then she realizes her upper lip is wet, and she laughs with the realization. He winks at her, and they carry on as siblings do.

—Izmir

The Guy in Sunglasses

He was his sunglasses. He could see perfectly well, but these were as much a part of his outfit as his long black ponytail. Reasonably, he wore the sunglasses while his children monopolized the swimming pool. Then he wore them in the lobby while reading the newspaper and chain-smoking. He wore them in the morning as he cut in front of other people waiting for tea and drained the last drops without compassion. He wore them in the dinner buffet line as he pointed to the fish he wanted and the chicken he did not.

However, heading to check out, he thoughtlessly propped his shades on the top of his head. As he crossed the hotel hallway, his eyes showed. He didn't look around while dragging his huge suitcase down the narrow passage. He did not yield to anyone, thus forcing the other guests to flatten themselves against the walls as he thundered through.

Without his shades, one could see his eyes when he tripped down the set of stairs that led to the lobby. It meant the brothers and sisters tiring of ping-pong and the women waiting for their husbands, and the employees with nothing to do could see him completely.

He stretched forward, lunged, trying to find the ground beneath him. When he caught his balance and was no longer in danger of falling, his eyes flashed and he became a little boy without many friends. He looked like any kid without a place to sit in the lunchroom. Maybe even the British woman whose toes were casualties of his suitcase would reconsider her curses if she saw him there, jerking his sunglasses over his flushed face as he marched for the exit.

—Ölüdeniz

Not a Drop of Worry

A tall father rushed to keep his tiny daughter under their umbrella, trying to watch the fellow pedestrians so as not to gouge them, and also trying to watch the girl he so clearly adored as she jumped over and into puddles. He stepped along, wary of the countless ways to break one's ankle on Istanbul streets and sidewalks. In one moment, he sighed upward at the God that would create both daughters and rain, and a crowded street full of holes, restless pedestrians, boys roasting chestnuts and men smoking cigarettes.

They needed to rush to catch the tram, so he picked her up. He hoisted her sideways under his arm, head forward and legs kicking behind, as his daughter laughed with delight in their sprint of the final paces to the turnstile. Once there, he had to set her down and use his pass to enter, use both hands to close their umbrella, but she kept her arms up, grinning at the face far above her, waiting to be carried further on.

—Istanbul

Palms

Two small boys track the line of workers trimming the palm trees. The men in green jumpsuits stare up at the man-lift. The boys nod at each other with tight-lipped smiles and start in motion. The slightly smaller of the boys unfolds the large package in his hand. He takes out a gruesome mask—a green and red face, half pig and half monster. The mask has a tuft of black hair at the top. He tugs the rubber mask over his face, despite the August heat, and roars as he approaches the first few workers.

Large fronds fall around the men and the boys, and most of the men ignore the growling, gaze right over the boys' heads, watch women passing by, or sometimes briefly glance at their work. Finally a man near the middle, caught off guard, gives a small leap and a double-take on account of the costumed boy. The boy's unmasked friend is delighted! Success! The friend wants a high five, but the mask blocks the other boy's peripheral vision, so the celebration settles into a solo fist pump. Though they only come up to the elbows of the men chopping the palm trees, the boys rush away triumphant, as though they could have done the job without the lift.

—Istanbul

Grasping at Grandmas

Early in my language learning I had a mission: to get old Turkish ladies to like me. I love elderly people, but I wasn't getting a warm reception when I beamed at the grandmas. I greeted little old ladies leaning out of their windows in the morning, little old ladies carrying produce, little old ladies in the market as they purchased four eggs and I blushingly purchased thirty. (It's difficult enough to explain a "protein window" in English, let alone to one's minuscule neighbor at the store.)

Usually, the dear gals gazed right past me or gave a faint smile and a nod. On occasion my happy "Merhaba" was met in kind, but for the most part, the little old ladies remained aloof. One did come out of her shell at the train station in Izmir, telling me never to trust my boyfriend as she had never trusted her husband. With a faint smile, I caught the next train.

One day, I sat in a collection of four benches on the path between the Archaeological Museum and the Topkapi Palace. It was in the shade and a good place to scrawl in my notebook as visitors came and went. A Korean man sat on the bench next to me, studying his map. An old Turkish woman in a headscarf and Dolce & Gabbana sunglasses took the bench on my left. On the far right bench, another old woman in a headscarf and long coat joined us. The Far woman asked me in Turkish where I was from and I answered this softball question without incident. She continued to ask questions I could reasonably answer, and I was pleased to practice. The Near woman chatted with me as well, in a quick pace, until I told her–she closer and with better hearing–that my Turkish wasn't so great, so please pardon me if I didn't always understand. She slowed her pace of speech almost in time with the Far woman speeding up. Far would compose frolicking monologues that I answered with a helpless shake of my head. Near seemed to tell Far that I wasn't fluent in Turkish, but Far only said, "Eh?" And she went on talking without a break.

The Korean man said with surprise, "You speak Turkish," and as I admitted my lack of skill, the conversation picked up around us. The man and I turned politely left, then right, then left, in a veritable tennis match of words I didn't know. The Near woman still stumping me from time to time, despite speaking slowly, and the Far woman growing farther away as she requested details and I kept answering: "Yes, I think so too."

Despite missing the mark in conversation, both women smiled over me. I knew enough to politely accept compliments on my green eyes. I knew enough to ask with interest about their children. And as Near's family came to collect her, she wouldn't depart before showing off her tiny grandson—who I'd apparently heard a lot about today. He was coy at first but ultimately posed for a picture. It's always a joy to make inroads with the recalcitrant.

—Istanbul

CKSON

ERS

Love

It's such an early shuttle to the airport. Two young brothers wear green plaid shirts, gray sandals, black cargo pants in larger and smaller sizes respectively. Groggy as they board, their mother directs them to a set of seats and takes the free place next to me, across the aisle from the boys. She glances over at them before her head drops back and her eyes close.

The boys are incredibly tired. The older leans against the window. The younger tilts his face upward and closes his eyes. Still his lashes flutter and his face scrunches in concentration, as though trying to will himself to sleep. The lane changes from the driver—as well as a few sudden tests of the brakes—keep the boys from settling in.

The older brother is frustrated and rubbing his eyes, when the smaller boy pats his own knee. Older brother lies down with his head across his little brother's legs, finally able to relax. The now-pillow-boy sits very still, holding his hands back so as not to disturb the bigger boy's nap.

I'm grinning over this scene when the little one slowly turns toward me. He notices my gaze and raises an eyebrow, giving me a minuscule "Are you lookin' at me?" expression. It briefly makes me smile even more, but I cover my mouth. Then I back down and look away, minding my own business, as the victor in our exchange sits up straighter and watches his brother sleep.

—Istanbul

Pick Me Up

The Taksim bus station, night and day, hosts chaos. Buses line up and depart from four doubled-up lines and feature the soundtrack of air brakes and honking horns. Pedestrians, as they aim to navigate the traffic and the taxis, test their nerve through exhales of cigarette smoke and inhales of diesel exhaust.

The 35C Kocamustafapaşa bus arrives but pauses a few feet away. The doors are closed as the driver stands slowly from his seat, and shuffles to check his domain. He moves toward the rear seats looking for stray passengers or purchases, any items left behind. On his way, he stops, reaches up to the hand straps and performs a few pull-ups. He snaps off four or five, crunches his knees in toward his protruding belly, makes a face to himself in the effort. He stops and stretches in pride. He takes a few more steps, then tries again, another set of pull-ups with mixed success. The passengers outside busy themselves with impatience. He brushes down his blue-button up shirt, adjusts the two pens in his front pocket, and returns to his wheel. He drives forward to the waiting passengers. As the doors sigh open, he strokes his mustache and nods, amped for the route ahead.

—Istanbul

Hats Off

He tumbles, his small souvenir fez cap flying. The boy and his younger sister had been running down the cobblestones by the Archaeology Museum, dashing on ahead of their parents. After he falls, his toddling sister stops cold. She leans over her brother. He is slow to stand and holds the side of his head, but he does not cry. She is half his height but leans down since he remains low to the ground. She presses her souvenir over her ears—a headband made from a string of cloth flowers—then she collects her brother's keepsake. The fez is dusted off in an instinctual brushing before she hands it over. She touches the uninjured side of his head just as he begins to feel the attention is too much. He chokes back tears as their parents finally approach, and lifts himself to stand tall. Still worried about her big brother, but somehow understanding the limits of an ego, the girl carefully follows, patting his elbow only when no one is looking.

—Istanbul

On Gratitude

It is an intensely long line at passport control. Flights keep arriving and people keep cutting. A tall man and I are both determined to stick to the vaguely orderly queue, though streams of people march to the front without waiting. The tall man says, "We must be the Americans. Single-file like a pair of suckers." We aren't even into the maze of silver bars yet. It's been 20 minutes and we've moved about four steps.

A family from India stands in front of us, also waiting, until they see that we're next to an open space that would put us ahead of the mob, if we would climb between two low bars. At least we could stem the tide. The father mutters it to the grandmother. Their set of boys in matching striped shirts stare at the opening as their elders contemplate the move. We should go ahead of the people ignoring the line, after all. It would be just! Grandma is remarkably spry. She hustles through first, then father, the boys, their mother. The tall man from California nudges me to follow suit. He also steps through. We're at least in the labyrinth now and the boys are delighted. The shorter of the two boys beams at me. "Come on! Let's break some rules!" Yet, there isn't much headway after that.

The wait is long and toasty. Slow steps of arriving passengers, glares toward people who had cut in front of us earlier, the unearthing of passports. I think of my father's grandparents who came to America on a boat from Sweden when they were children. I think of that authentically long journey, and remind myself that it is a gift to have ready access to a protein bar and clean socks. And to be able to go on a trip to Turkey in the first place, on a whim, via an airplane, with good books and an iPod.

A toddler girl in a flowered dress and red shoes stops the slow procession forward. She gives up, crosses her arms, and begins to cry. I know that feeling. I would have been with her before, but now I am too busy counting my blessings.

—Istanbul

Affection and Cargo

A line of tour buses waited outside the leather goods store. As tourists wandered in to admire coats and boots despite the 100-degree heat, their drivers scattered out—smoking, standing in the shade, chatting with their hands behind their backs, pacing in small circles. In the middle of the line, a bus had the luggage area wide open on both sides. There were no suitcases below, so with the cargo doors ajar a breeze rushed the hollow space. It created a convenient location to make a bed. The driver slept on his side, turned toward the road, with his palms together and tucked under his head, like a caricature of a sleeping child. His wife sat on the other side, away from the dust of the road, but she wasn't yet ready to rest.

She peered at him from over his shoulder. He was red-faced with an expansive belly, and her look displayed only tenderness. She reached out and hesitated. Her hand moved to smooth hair that was swept up by the wind of a passing car, but she paused and watched him breathe. Eventually, she surrendered to touching him on the shoulder lightly before leaning back. She arranged a pillow or two, propping herself up to watch the rise and fall of his ribs, already pleased to find herself in the middle of a nice dream.

—Selcuk

The Humbling Scenes: Part I

If you have a good sense of direction, please never forget that this is a gift. Like those who can sleep in airplanes, you have been granted something very beautiful. Be grateful for it.

In an attempt to familiarize myself with my new city, I walked for four hours and found none of the places I had planned to visit. I couldn't find a church I'd hoped to attend; I couldn't find two other sights on my list. I gave up the search after three hours. Then it took me another hour to get home.

Practicing my Turkish, I did ask for directions. I learned that if you ask ten people, two would admit they don't know, four would give vague or counter-productive directions because they didn't want to admit they didn't know, and four would give helpful instructions that I would be unable to follow or would swiftly forget. Everyone answered with a smile, at least.

Still eighty blocks from home, an older man said he knew the area, and he'd gladly walk me there. He also needed to ask; he also discovered that we received a lot of seemingly credible tips that led nowhere. At a café a man assured us that my place was right around the corner. Doubling back after the dead end, my guide said: "But that's not the right one, brother!" And the man at the café shrugged behind his cigarette.

By the time we found my street, I think the man was tired of my gratitude, "Thank you so much," "You're so kind," "I'll pray for you and your family." A gesture that seemed so slight turned into 30 minutes with a cheerful blonde on his heels. He smiled when we parted, but as he turned to go, he let out a huge sigh. I couldn't have agreed more.

—Izmir

The Humbling Scenes: Part II

I knew I couldn't walk to my Turkish class. I stared at a map and felt some vague hope that if I went to a metro station I knew, I could probably walk the rest of the way to the school. Perhaps. Just in case, I left 90 minutes early. However, to get in the metro, you need a special card, and I learned I couldn't buy that card at seven in the morning. A man at a fruit stand assured me that a bus driver would let me pay in cash. So I waited in a long line for a morning bus. I boarded and then learned that I could not, in fact, pay the driver.

I would have considered it a victory for my Turkish language skills to understand the driver, if he hadn't been sullenly saying, "If you don't have a card, don't get on the bus. Get out." Piles of people were pouring in behind me, and I had no way to return to the street. A woman in the front row handed me her card to use, and despite her protests, I gave her the change the driver wouldn't take. She had no idea what this meant to me, but the tears in my eyes led her to accept the change. Later I watched her glare at the driver in the mirror above his seat. God bless her.

I moved to the back and stood shoulder to shoulder with other passengers, and I had to ask a woman where I should get out of the bus. She kept saying the names of stations, which I didn't recognize as stations, and I gave her a lot of smiles while thinking, "I'm just going to have to take a taxi." Another woman noted my glazed panic, recognized my school, and walked me to the proper street before going off to her job for the day.

It had been a while, to be honest, since I had been so lost in a city. I'd gotten into the habit of going to places I knew, where I could navigate a city without having to ask anyone, and where I knew what to expect. Here, I am foreign again. I have to be humble and allow others to have mercy on me. They did so with kindness, and my need reminded me to be grateful. This is also a part of finding my way.

—Izmir

Unsuspecting

In a row of souvenir shops by the Hagia Sofia, a tiny girl with blonde curls wanders ahead of her mother, who has been enjoying the distractingly flirtatious salesmen. The mother assesses a tapestry; the girl idly lifts a yellow ceramic shoe the length of her head. The keepsake is decorated with painted flowers and a scrawl of the word "Istanbul," which she squints over since she's too young to read. The girl tucks the shoe under her arm and moves on to the next storefront.

The salesman, not alarmed, holds his cigarette at his side and smirks at the girl's boldness. As her mother catches up, she gives him a knowing smile without knowing. He nods toward her child. The mother blinks, rebuffed for a moment until she realizes what she should have been supervising.

"Sam!" Our cold criminal gazes toward the sound of her name. "Come here. Will you come here?" The mother screeches and crosses to her unmoving daughter, who welcomes her mother with a half-shrug. "You can't just take that. That's almost like pinching!" The girl still doesn't hold up her acquisition, so the shoe is seized from her side. Our shoplifter appears amazed by her mother's discovery.

"It's very bad, almost pinching, don't you know that?" The mother returns the merchandise without eye contact or an apology. The salesman bows as he receives it, covering his grin. And the little girl wanders on to subsequent tables of souvenirs, already forgetting her lesson and wiggling her fingers.

—Istanbul

Window Shopping

No need to rush to the airport, two businessmen opt to take a coffee in the lobby of their hotel, where all of the signs are in English and Arabic. The only traces of Istanbul are the names on the waiter's lapels. They order cappuccinos. The men choose chairs by a plate glass window and chat over their carry-on luggage and loosened ties.

A man of equivalent age stops outside and sets down a large plastic sack. His business hours usually begin at dusk, but as a similarly savvy entrepreneur, he will not miss a chance to make a sale. Through the window, he starts the negotiations. He holds up a few of the imitation designer shirts: a polo shirt, a button up. Beautiful, beautiful, he says to the pristine glass.

The seated men try to look past him, pretend he isn't there. However, it is hard to miss how their graying temples match his, how their shoulders and bellies are similarly rounded. The inside men look down into the dregs of their half-empty cups and check their expensive watches. The man outside the window digs through the bag. He stands upright from his wares displaying one last option and a sly grin, insisting that they all knew quality when they see it.

—Istanbul

Kindred Kid

She is wearing a magenta rain jacket with floral buttons. She's probably in fourth grade, maybe fifth or sixth. She's been watching me out of the corner of her eye since she boarded the bus, eavesdropping on my conversation with a friend who wants to speak English while I answer in Turkish. We're both practicing, and sometimes breaking into the other language in the middle of a sentence. I meet the little girl's gaze and smile, but she looks away. She moves as people enter the bus, but she stays within earshot, tilting her head like a thoughtful adult. When her stop arrives, she hops down from the bus to meet her brother and begins to tell him about this odd, interesting conversation. She even turns to the bus, and as she points, she notices that I have turned in her direction as well. We grin at each other. Fellow people-watchers, happy curiosities, wishing each other good night.

—Izmir

Serenade for the Sheepish

From the moment she and her husband are seated, they eat and drink in silence. They don't discuss the menu. They order by pointing. He looks through photos on his phone. She tucks her hair behind her ear, glances briefly at passersby, or stares into space.

A trio of musicians has been sitting at the bar, waiting for a few more patrons, until finally they stood as a group and began to play at different tables. The first to receive a close-proximity performance is a table with a set of female tourists, middle-aged and blonde, unsmiling even when the music is up-tempo. The second table is more delighted. They are a crew of six who try to sing along.

As the musicians move toward the mute pair, she folds her arms, then unfolds them, then folds them again, then fiddles with her silverware. Finally, she shyly poses for her husband's video capture of this slightly embarrassing moment. Despite her body language protests, despite her nervousness during the approach, she gives in. She accepts the odd situation and the certainty of being a tourist. She smiles. She offers up her first unabashed smile of the evening. The musicians sing and she seems relieved when they leave, but as the trio wanders away, she takes her husbands hands across the table. They laugh at the experience and lean in close to the phone, admiring his camerawork, watching the video over and over again.

—Istanbul

Wrinkles

I'm feeling connected. I'm feeling like the Trappist monk Thomas Merton when he left his monastery to go into the city and observed the frailty of all the activity there. Or I'm wishing to feel like Thomas Merton, and thus projecting. Either way, I'm grinning at everyone in the bus.

There's a woman riding this morning who is surely ancient. I've never seen a face like hers before. She wears a remarkable set of wrinkles, like a gathered curtain around her eyes. I watch her looking out the windows and observing the people who enter. She doesn't seem frail, but hearty and grounded instead. She has me thinking about what my lines will be if I get to reach a drapery age.

Will my wrinkles come from laughter with my friends? Which lines from the gasps over a beautiful passage in a book? Will my lines come from crying over heartaches that I have later forgotten? Which from the scowl at a hard passage of philosophy? Which from the grief of losing people that I love? I wonder as I watch her, with a delight instead of a lament, how I may also grow older and what it might reveal on my face. How will I develop and how will I fold?

—Izmir

Benim Kızım and Other Cures for Airsickness

A general rustling of reading material echoes through the airplane. Everyone shifts in their place, digs through the belongings that should be stowed under the seat. The whole middle section of passengers tries to make noise, if nothing else, to block their ears from the sounds in aisle 16.

A beautifully made-up woman—pink floral headscarf and narrowly plucked eyebrows—spends the twenty minutes after take-off vomiting. Flight attendants remain in their seats. Her mother perches beside her. The old woman wraps her skirt over her once-young legs as she tucks those legs under her in the seat. They are a birdlike pair, though it is hard to identify the bird—pheasant, peacock, egret—some undefined class of bird, learned back in elementary school. The mother glares around to see if anyone is disturbed by her daughter's evident distress, then consoles her embarrassed adult daughter by calling her my child, my darling, my little girl.

—Flight from Chicago to Istanbul

I Want to Tell You Something Beautiful

After a few weeks practicing my Turkish with various strangers, I'm pleased with my progress—but overwhelmed by how much I still have to learn. Smiling helps. Smiling helps me make inroads. Especially when I have done well for a few sentences and gain confidence, then I aim for a full paragraph that loses my listener. I'm unintentionally cracking people up all the time.

I wait for the day when I can be funny on purpose. When I feel like the person speaking will actually be me. When I can say something true, something weighty, something lovely.

—Izmir

Totally Not Making This Up

The salesman gazes and grins at a tourist sitting alone in the outdoor café. Her chair points toward his shop. To investigate him, she looks across the center of a table where two ladies with large, elaborate earrings examine menus. The tourist smiles across at the salesman. He waves, she waves back.

One of the ladies in the earrings turns to her purse for make-up. Lunch will remove her lip-gloss, so she adds more eye shadow, more blush. One shouldn't look unkempt while eating soup. As she makes herself up, she catches the solo tourist gesturing but notes it is not her attention being sought, only some fixed point beyond her table. The lady turns in the direction of the action so slowly that the salesman has walked away. He wanders around his booth, turning toward his admirer at times, and then walking off to smirk over his luck. In one moment he would toss over a long stare or a wave of invitation to tea, and then he would move behind a belly dancer costume and disappear from view.

The accompanied lady notes the solo one smiling at a point in space where the salesman paces around, but the lady never turns her jewelry-laden neck quickly enough to see his side of their communication. Beneath her blush and over her lunch, she begins to wonder if perhaps this lonely solo is a bit crazy?

Solo knows quite well that the accompanied lady never catches her new friend's advances. She takes delight in carrying on, just to make the made-up lady's face pleat with curiosity. At one point, Solo holds up both hands and mouths "ten minutes" as she yields to the smiles of the salesman. The accompanied lady swallows her omelet and whispers to her companion that the lonely one seems very strange. Her lady friend checks, then titters in agreement.

Later, the make-up table observes Solo walking away, but they wither a bit when the salesman hurries out to greet her. The ladies accompany each other then, moving in unison, touching napkins to the corners of their mouths and reaching for their mirrors. If they re-tell the story at home, they will leave out this resolution, this run-of-the-mill flirting. It is far more interesting to have spotted a madwoman on one's summer vacation.

—Istanbul

Seek and You Will Find

The grandson at full height comes to his grandfather's knees, but he speaks looking straight up as though it's the most ordinary way to hold a conversation. Baba smiles down at him as the boy describes something exciting. Then the boy makes a proclamation and turns to a nearby pole, away from Grandpa, covering his eyes and counting slowly. When he gets to ten, he turns. His grandfather is still beaming over at him. "Grandpa," the boy scolds.

"Oh! You found me!" The man calls back in great surprise. "How clever you are! You found me!" The boy laughs, and Grandpa remains in place as the patient countdown begins again.

—Izmir

Big Sister

The morning bus is packed, and I am standing in the baby-carriage corral near the front. There aren't many parents rolling their babies on board at this hour, so it has become my usual place to stand. A young girl reaches for the rail in front of me. She comes up to my chin. As the bus continues to fill up, I aim to protect her by taking up a bit more space—straightening my posture, pushing out my handbag with my shoulder—creating an area where she will have enough room to stand. Under my shadow, she looks up and smiles at me. I think it is universal that people are not smiling at 7:30 am in any given bus, but we are happy and trading glances every few minutes until I depart. "Iyi dersler," I wish her a nice day at her studies and she turns to wave.

The next day, we're on the same bus again. She comes to stand next to me and we grin like old friends. We try some chit-chat. She is in high school, studying logistics. She will go on to the university. She is the only child of a taxi driver and a homemaker. I tell her about my sisters and my brother. She compliments my Turkish, right after a sentence I have struggled to compose. Her name is Ece and she says now she has an older sister as well. Yes, it is a wonderful thing to have a sister.

—Izmir

Baby's First Swim

The mother slowly hands her infant to his father, who waits in the shallow end of the hotel swimming pool. The baby wears a diaper and a cloth head-wrap like a chef. Grandma sits by patiently, with an expectant hope that she'll be needed. The baby fusses and cries as his legs enter the water. Yet, the father holds his son, smiling and making happy faces to help his boy to keep calm. The baby's torso twists above the water as he weeps. His mother flinches, stretches to take him back, but the father blinks in reassurance.

Watching baby's first dips are his family and a cast of guests, including a couple in love who tread together in the deep end. In lounge chairs: a British man covered in gray chest-belly-shoulder-hair and suntan oil, a man with a daiquiri, a girl holding up a fashion magazine. But everyone has openly broken from their reveries, their romantic gazes, their trend-seeking, in order to catch the baby shifting from tears to giggles. From anxious first kicks to yielding. The baby clings closer while his father walks safely across the pool, holding the child aloft. The leisurely observers laugh as the baby strikes the water with a joyful fist, a mark of new triumph, a fear overcome.

—Ölüdeniz

Tram Nap

The Kabataş tram sighs through an intersection and a boy stops short to let it pass. He waits with some annoyance, until he discovers something in the last car. A man in a button-up shirt, briefcase in his lap, slumps against the window, snoozing. The boy's eyes flash. As the car rolls by, the boy pounces. He slaps the glass of the window, spinning quickly to see the reaction of the man he's awakened, the man jolting upright and trying to place himself.

In the next seat, a reverently-old man laughs, pats his groggy neighbor's shoulder, permitting the other passengers to trade glances with quiet delight. A pair of young girls giggle into their mother's long skirt. Then the tram picks up speed and the riders return to their reveries, still wearing fractions of smiles.

—Istanbul

The Joy of Forgetting

This morning I took my notebook to the park. I had a delightful time running a pen dry. While taking notes on what I've seen this week, I suddenly started writing a passage in Turkish. Sometimes it's easier to write about your feelings when the results will be necessarily banal. My grasp of Turkish adjectives is still slim. This week I worked on nice goal words: "generous," "friendly," and "brave."

Nonetheless, when I check out the Turkish passage now, I look forward to two different moments ahead. 1.) The day I can read it and smile at my grammatical errors. 2.) The day I won't be able to read it, but will remember that once I did what so many claim they want to do—I tore off after a big adventure.

The Turkish language will most likely disappear from my part-of-the-brain-made-for-languages-but-already-sadly-full-of-80s-pop-songs. Yet, I hope I will recall feeling very blessed and grateful.

—Istanbul

Mr. Independent

A little boy in a blue t-shirt acts tough, strong, fearless. He clutches a toy truck low at his side and eyes the passengers on the train. His father sees a friend near the front of the car, and moves away to talk to him. The boy breaks free of his mother's grasp to follow his father, to meet the acquaintance, to get another view of the crowd. He travels up on the toes of his rubber shoes.

The boy studies a few children in the car with a raised eyebrow, an expression his father shares. Nearby sit a boy about his age and twin girls with white skirts and sequins. His mother calls, "Gel!" *Come.* In her direction he tosses a dismissive movement, another mannerism lifted from his father.

As the boy scans the crowd, he spots two elderly women with their heads covered. He gasps and backs up to his father, but seems drawn to keep returning and peering at them. One woman blinks at him, then waves her fingers, and he stumbles backward. He hustles away as the women chuckle.

A few minutes later he continues his observations. As though he'd forgotten they were there, he spots the women, panics, and flees again. Now the amusement is contagious. The women laugh, boy's father apologizes quietly and laughs; the friend laughs, the children laugh. Finally, the boy laughs too, not sure why. He joins in until he again spots the mysteriously scary women and rushes straight to his mother.

—Izmir

What We Deserve

He is a terror. He keeps kicking the trash cans that are on hinges, so they screech and rock forward and back. His mother has been trying to pray a bit; his father has been filling up water at the spring. So, briefly left to his own devices, the boy has been trying to disturb as many trash can targets as possible. His mother calls for him to stop, warns that he is going to get hurt. He runs through crowds of tourists, cutting around them, making them stagger their steps, trip over each other, drop their guidebooks. They glare at him. Tiny as he is, he inspires a hearty disdain in the strangers around him.

When he falls, when he scrapes his knee, the tourists glance away. One woman raises an eyebrow and smirks, vindicated that the boy gets what he deserves, for being so rude and so reckless. His mother's prediction came true, and the woman exchanges a look with her companions.

Yet, his mother goes straight to him. She gathers him up from the ground, tends to his knee. He goes silent in her arms. She tells him he should have listened, but she whispers it, a kind rebuke, as she embraces her son in love.

—Ephesus

Watch Your Step

Thank you, Lord, that I spotted the three little old ladies in their long skirts and head scarves recoiling in horror at the prospect of riding an airport escalator. It was excellent.

They were in a group of five, the three women and two men. The third woman let the other two ladies step on with giggles, gathering their skirts and holding each other in the descent. The men joined them, but without the giggling.

The third woman's scarf was beige with flowers. She refused to join the others on the downward slope, moving out of the way of other travelers and eyeing the nearby up-escalator that was frozen in energy saver mode and resembled stairs. She briefly considered just walking down those. One of the men yelled—husband-like—as he rolled on ahead. The other man, perhaps her grown son, hiked up the down escalator to save her from herself. He let some impatient passengers pass, then led his mother carefully back on track. He stepped first; she followed quickly, without breathing. Then she clutched her skirt and shifted from foot to foot. As the end approached, she dug her fingers into her son's arm as he eased her onto firm ground. He wore a big smile, like a parent gazing at a child finally coaxed to eat their vegetables.

One more escalator ride stood between them and their gate. The husband-like man calling out, the two gigglers bounding ahead automatically, and the son speaking quietly with his mother to keep her mind elsewhere. By the second set of moving stairs, she had already grown less apprehensive. Her husband tried to hustle her but she stared beyond him. She stepped right on, haughty, not even looking down. She would come along as he called, but she wouldn't be caught enjoying herself.

—Istanbul

Manners

On the busy road, a taxi driver slows, inspiring a concerto of honking horns behind him. A red soccer ball rolls into traffic. I notice the children, the owners of the ball, a few blocks ahead, peering to see what might be the untimely conclusion of their game. Two girls, two boys, another girl holding a light pink ball and hugging it, perhaps as a sign that it would be unfit for their match.

A man hustles out into traffic to retrieve the ball. He looks down the block and sees how far it has rolled from the children. I offer to deliver it, as I am walking in their direction anyway. He pauses with the hesitation of an ego considering kicking the ball to show off his prowess, then thankfully he chooses the second option: bringing it a few paces and not punting the ball at the foreign blonde woman. I carry it closer to where the children stand, and one small boy slides down the side of the hill in a rush to accept it. He keeps his head low, "Teşekkür ederim." Graciously thanking me for bringing back their afternoon, he runs back to his friends, all waving and whispering thank yous, so I can practice the phrase from the Turkish conversation books, "Bir şey değil."

It was nothing.

—Istanbul

You Can Read Over My Shoulder, But You Can't Come Along

In the shuttle bus to the airplane, I break into scraps of conversational Turkish with a group of teenage boys from Kahramanmaraş. Even the boldest among them, a boy with smooth hair and light eyes, is subject to bolts of shyness. They are at the closing of a school trip, and remain curious—asking me about my Turkish boyfriend in simple phrases, often repeating themselves over and over until I get a general idea of the topic. Or until I make a wild stab at a sentence, hoping that my answer might relate to their question. They often divide into small groups and confer, then one representative returns with a new inquiry.

In the airplane, I have an aisle seat across from the light-eyed one, who continues his attempts at chatting across the aisle. In the window seat of my row sits the boy who most resembles my cousin—sheepish and kind. He seems to have a better mastery of English but is too apprehensive to speak. He offers me a red apple with a smiling blink.

Somewhere after takeoff another from their group, newly splashed with cologne, takes the middle seat between my surrogate cousin and myself. He takes up the helpless interview until I politely nod and turn to my book.

I am reading Flannery O'Connor's Collected Short Stories, a book with peacock feathers on the front. I lean over a story called, "The Turkey," without thinking of any clever connection to my neighbors. I dig into this story while the three around me try to read along, even the one leaning across the aisle tries despite the interruptions of the beverage and duty-free carts.

A line from the story strikes me and I grow still. Tears drop from my eyes onto the book. The boys jump. They could see the English word for their country at the top of the page, but this may have been all they could discern from the story, written in dialect, and causing that happy American woman to grow so swept away and solitary.

—Flight from Budapest, Hungary to Istanbul

Stories from Austria

For the (Mean) Professor Who Told Me to be Realistic

On a brilliant November day, my students talked me into teaching outside. So we were at an outdoor amphitheater on the Danube River when I broke into the story of a professor on my Christmas card list. In college, I spent summers in a small town in Colorado working as a waitress at a sports bar and restaurant. Waiting tables is good penance and a particular sort of training to endure life's haters.

A couple came in one day and we visited while the wife mulled the beer list. The man asked what I was studying, what I wanted to do. He caught me in a hopeful spirit. I'd just taken a literature course that renewed my faith in reading, in something I'd loved since childhood. I said I might like to be an English professor one day. His wife gazed away and the man scoffed. He was himself an English professor at a nearby university and when they had one vacancy that year, they received over 200 applications. "So perhaps," he recommended, "you should consider those odds."

The whole experience was just as vivid when I disclosed the story to my students. I fumed that I wanted to send him a Christmas card, a reminder of what he'd said. That prof went about eating his meal while my 19-year-old self had to fight to keep from crying. I'd never had a stranger leave me so deflated, so upset.

As I admitted my anger in the tale, I dropped my copy of "Microserfs," the book I'd assigned. It fell from my hands and collapsed onto the sidewalk below me. My student Miloš raised his hand quickly. Miloš: charming and shy, kind and distracted, but this story had his attention. I reached down to recover the book as in his Serbian-toned English he said, "Hey, in my country, if someone is speaking and they drop something, or there's a crash or a loud noise—that means it's true. It's really true."

A few other students had similar traditions, so they nodded as well. Agreeing that what they heard was the truth. And so it was. While that professor likely toiled away grading composition papers and crushing dreams, I stood on the banks of the Danube teaching Douglas Coupland to students from nine different countries. And perhaps he was right to tell me to be realistic about my odds, and to crush that dream, so I could go about exceeding it.

So, Merry Christmas, Professor. May the year take you by surprise and shift your spirit. I wish the same for my students and for all waitstaff I encounter.

With love from Vienna, Paige

En Garde

Runaways from a political rally, two helium balloons clap together. They are entangled above an intersection, caught in a wire on the side of an apartment. A man in a cardigan leans out of his third story window to glare at these balloons. He reaches his arm out to release them, to no avail, and disappears back inside.

Soon he returns. With a fireplace poker.

He sets to work, holding himself against the window frame with one arm as he fences his adversaries with the other. It's unclear if he is dismayed by the political leanings of the balloons or bothered their trespassing. With a great stretch, he catches one and it pops–the sound of success drowned out by a departing bus.

A beautiful woman with a grocery bag of vegetables stands below the scene. She notices a few her fellow pedestrians staring at something above her. She looks up slowly, trying to make her curiosity appear like the typical upward stretch of a slightly tired, still beautiful woman. But then she gasps and dashes off in startled jaywalking. Clearly, she doesn't trust the man's grip on his potentially deadly fireplace implement.

With one last jab, he finally bursts the second balloon. He makes a small noise of joy. A crowd of schoolchildren on the sidewalk give him a round of brief, sarcastic applause. He gazes down upon them, victorious nonetheless, and continues to smile to himself as he closes his window.

—Vienna

Not Helpless

I was trudging home from an English lesson with my astounding student, an asylum seeker and former child soldier from Sierra Leone, who had the most remarkably shy smile. He could speak English well, but he was now learning to read and to write. He knew the Koran by heart, but from the first day he had to concentrate to write his name. Given his love for the Chelsea soccer club, this was another of the first words he labored to write during our sessions.

On that particular day, he'd talked about a time when he could go home, become a good leader to the people of his country. This was by far the most ambitious dream he'd voiced. Most of the time he talked about finding a kind wife, starting a family, and then teaching his children to play soccer. The explanation of it always put a lump in my throat. Such a simple dream made almost impossible as he waited year after year for on a decision about his asylum case.

As I made my way home, I went through the usual frustration about feeling helpless to provide him much more than an hour of distraction each week. An elderly woman approached with a toddler in a stroller, coming down the sidewalk toward me, directing the child's attention as they moved. "Is that a tree or a flower?" "A tree!" "Is that a woman or a girl?" "A woman!" I would like to have been called a girl, seen as so terrifically young, but I still smiled at them as they moved on to the next objects. "Is that a bicycle or a motorcycle?" And so on.

I stopped in a shop to continue my hunt for wide-lined writing paper without cartoons on the front. I wanted to give our lessons some age-appropriate dignity. I wanted to show him I was also grateful for the chance to sit with him and hear his hopes for the future. Maybe our first steps are always small ones. Even these do seem to lead us somewhere.

—Vienna

Morning Routine

A woman on her balcony turns her back to the street and raises her arms in a wide V overhead. She stretches at her reflection in the balcony windows. She reaches for the sky again, twice more, then bounces in a set of jumping jacks, her arms move up and down, her perfectly styled bun unmoving. She wears a long-sleeved black shirt and observes her lean leaping frame in the windows, quitting after a brief, invigorating set.

She turns to face the street and delicately lifts a white mug to her lips. A moment later, she replaces the mug with a toothbrush and cleans her teeth overlooking the street. From time to time, she spits into the boxes of plants and flowers that line her elegant balcony. She sips from the mug, brushes, and spits. Over and over.

I spot her from below, standing on the platform as I wait for the U4 subway train. During the jumping jacks, I rifle through in my bag for my notebook and pen. As I scrawl her morning routine, a couple to my left gaze up to see what I see, step a bit to the right to get a better view. An old man who fails to read over my shoulder finally looks up to see for himself. We spend five minutes waiting for a delayed train, watching the thorough public toothbrushing. Unaware of her audience, the woman moves inside. As her balcony door closes, our train arrives, and we go our separate ways.

—Vienna

A Seat of One's Own

A boy and his little brother—each armed with a sack of groceries—board the bus and rush to pile into a single vacant seat. The younger boy's brown eyes flash as he wriggles to fit between the window and his slightly older, seemingly wiser, clearly more serious sibling. A woman on the aisle seat beside them, wearing a leopard print coat and a black hat with flowers, stares dead ahead and refuses to yield an inch to the children.

People rest in their thoughts or in faraway stares, until their stop, until they can continue their worrying in a less confined area. A similarly distracted woman across from the boys rises for her stop. She carefully guides herself past the collection of feet, dogs, and bags of produce that line her exit.

In a move of instinct, the smaller brother bolts to the open space and makes a show of the luxuriousness of his new location. He climbs up and pats the seat cushion on either side of his tiny legs; he kicks out the feet that no longer touch the floor, he stretches his arms wide—with a wingspan so narrow that he could barely touch either the window on his right or the annoyed passenger on his left. The older brother breaks his own grown-up gaze to offer an approving nod, making himself more comfortable as well. The small brother smiles in the direction of the window, though he can barely see out, and hugs the sack of bread to his chest in satisfaction.

—Vienna

Solo

In the small café, one has to adapt to custom and share a table with a stranger. I receive a welcome from a woman with hip glasses and excellent posture. She is Gisela, a retired teacher from Linz. She taught biology. And drama. This makes me grin, which makes her grin. She is visiting Vienna alone and stopped here for a relatively okay coffee, which she sips on for nearly 40 minutes.

We begin speaking German but without my noticing, she shuffles us into English. Probably for the best. She came to Vienna for a week while her husband went to a trade show. She delights in not having to ask anyone where to go, or what to do. She sighs a little and says I probably get to enjoy that every day—as a single woman. Since I am so accustomed to making my own choices I wouldn't even notice how free I really am. We smile again at each other and gaze out at the city unaccompanied.

—Vienna

Good, But No Samaritan

On the 92A bus, a gruff Austrian soldier keeps his backpack on as he watches intently for his stop. Two elementary-aged boys on board spot an opportunity and sneak up next to the soldier. They connect a loop from his pack to a plastic strap at the empty wheelchair-accessible seat. The boys await the soldier's stop with ill-concealed glee. They ride beyond their exit in anticipation, whispering about riding the line back again. The soldier stays oblivious, staring out the window, and when he rings for his stop, the boys can barely contain themselves. As the doors open, the soldier is shocked. He's stuck, moving forward but being held back.

I reach over and free him—no Samaritan since I'd seen what the kids were up to and smirked along with them. At the next block, the boys fly out the doors in triumph. An old man commiserates with me about harmless children and we permit each other full, open, public laughter. The others in the bus stay quiet and serious, but we keep laughing until the last stop. Three years later, I recall the boys and laugh even now.

—Vienna

Slapstick Grandma

She offers her grandchildren a bright, rainbow umbrella. She opens it for those cherubs—a boy and a girl in galoshes—and lets the girl hold it over them both. She follows with a smart navy blue umbrella of her own. She smiles over her grandchildren. The rain doesn't change their day; they are out on a walk with Grandma just as planned. It's a peaceful time together.

The rain isn't too serious. However, up above, a gutter is clogged. Just a few meters ahead water pours in a stream onto the sidewalk. Grandma spies the temptation. "Nee, nee," she's giving them a no, anticipating their plan to test the umbrella under the splash. The small ones have picked up their pace and Grandma follows, continuing her warning, hustling to catch them. At the last moment, they obey. They step out of the tempting waterfall.

Yet, Grandma's protective momentum leads her onward, right under the shower, which blasts buckets of water over her thankfully hearty umbrella. The children gasp in glee, "Oooooo!" Surprised as she is, her laughter echoes up the narrow street. Grandma gets to have all the fun.

—Vienna

Self-Sufficient

An elementary-aged girl pushed the button for the tram to stop, then turned to her birdcage, which she had propped on a nearby seat. She exhaled and prepared herself with a nod at the window, at the floor. Inside were two disquieted parakeets. With a consoling whisper, she adjusted a sheet over the cage and stretched her arms wide. When the car lurched to halt, she steadied herself, then hoisted them up. The cage was the width of her wingspan. She peered over the top, her heavy shoes patting their way toward the stairs, her fingers reddening.

She made a small gasp of effort to stay upright, but no one moved to her aid. The twitch of her nose, the line of her brow revealed she was grateful that everyone kept to themselves. She rode the tram alone, she buttoned up her jacket, and she was the mother of these birds, after all. She made her way out and marched off with small grunts of effort, not taking a break, carrying on. Though the bystanders didn't stand to help, they did watch thoughtfully over her departure: the doors jerky, the stairs steep, and the strangers gazing over this small determination making an exit.

—Vienna

When All the German Fell Out of my Head

In every tunnel, because the darkness turns the windows into mirrors, people in the train gaze at their own reflection. They pose, pat their hair, examine their own eyes. As we break from one tunnel and the sun returns, an elderly man delights in the beams and stretches like a cat.

My neighbors begin to chat with me, observing that I have been writing in my notebook for nearly an hour. Now, I understand German pretty well until someone speaks to me. Then my ears get hot and I forget everything. I want to reply, but the anxiety of making mistakes upends any vocabulary I've acquired. The articles Der, Die, and Das melt away.

I fumble a bit and go mute. At least I don't have to tell anyone that I've been trying to learn German for a year and a half. Hopefully, they will assume I started only last week. We should go with that.

A little boy across the aisle notices that I am unable to speak. He peers at me over his pastry, then he smiles. I recognize that look of consolation. I give it to people who have tripped in public. But this boy buoys me. I smile back. I accept the kind gazes of the German speakers around me. I accept the gestures they make to communicate wordlessly that I should eat the apple they offer, that I should show them my ticket and they will tell me when to exit. I keep my grip on a shy expression and let my neighbors play hospitable charades.

Later the boy points his mother in my direction, then they both blink at me with mercy. I try to savor this chance to be utterly humbled. Vielen Dank. (I think.)

—In the train from Vienna to Innsbruck

Visiting Hours

At the prison outside Vienna, the visiting room is an open space: a sort of junior high craft room with long tables and church-like wooden benches. There is no glass partition to keep visitors from inmates, so greetings, hugs, handholding are all permitted. Outside, horses graze and farm trucks deliver the onions prisoners clean for a minuscule monthly income. It is a beautiful, clear day for staring out the windows.

A nervous inmate with a large, looped tattoo at the back of his neck, white-blue eyes, and markedly yellow teeth greets three male members of his family. The resemblances are obvious among the father, the inmate, and the two younger brothers. They trade handshakes and back thumps. His father's hand lingers on his shoulder. Slow conversation carries on in German after the hellos. The inmate looks to the guard for permission. He receives a nod before he passes a wrapped snack cake to his small brother, who sits between their father's oxygen tank and the other, morose middle brother.

The inmate and his brothers pull their long sleeves over their hands, shove them up, then tug them down again in a non-verbal chorus. The little brother looks around before opening the cake quietly and consuming it quickly. The inmate takes the wrapper back and crumples it tightly in his hand, smiling over his visitors for just a moment, before each returns to searching for anything to say.

—Hollabrun

It Takes One to Waltz

A boy in a hooded sweatshirt tips back his generic energy drink, then pauses under the illuminated sign for a dance studio. In the window, a display of streamers and course times surround a TV showing a video of woefully amateur couples in a ballroom dancing class. The duos step woodenly in wrong directions. Their eyes turn away from their partners to plead with their toes, to search for a space on the wall and count invisible numbers. The instructor walks between the hapless pairs, often leaping out of their way. No music is heard, only evening traffic. The boy stares at the screen without smirking. The dancers continue to crash.

The boy snaps to attention as a group of tipsy tourists approach. He finishes his beverage, shifts his feet wider apart, his shoulders down, his attention to the sidewalk. When the people pass, laughing and leaning into each other, the boy moves away from the yellow glow of the sign. He heads onward, taking light and careful steps for an almost unnoticeable moment before picking up his pace.

—Vienna

A Love Story at Just Under Five Feet

The elderly couple hunches together over their soup. They stay like this, heads tilted toward each other, even as they finish. The waiter reaches under the bridge of their gaze to withdraw their empty bowls. They only see each other. The rest of the world has its young posture, but they sit with their elbows on their laps.

Neither fixes the back of their hair, so they also share the marks of a heavy rest. It's like the Turkish phrase: *Allah sizi bir yastıkta kocatsın.* In my vague apologetic translation I'll say that's something akin to: May God let you grow old on the same pillow. Or with the same absent-minded pillow hair, perhaps.

When they get up to leave, he stands straight and waves across at the waiter. They will see each other again soon. She uses a cane and remains hunched. It is her way. Half is her highest height. He comes around to clear a chair from her path. Then, because he loves her, he will also lean down to keep her horizon as they exit into the street.

—Vienna

There's No Crying in the Vienna Airport

I'm crying in the airport. Just returning from a trip, feeling a bit overwhelmed with heartbreak, it is nice to be back in familiar Vienna. I know how to get to the S-Bahn station for a train to the city. At the ticket machine, tears stream down my face. It's out of character for me to weep openly in public, but it's also very hard to keep your belongings upright, dig for Euro change, and mop up tears at the same time–so I just let 'em roll.

A young Spanish guy interrupts. He asks in scraps of English how to get a ticket for the city center, how to use the machine if he can't speak German. Though it's normal for people to stop me, talk to me, I thought that today tears would deter conversation and allow me to wallow in peace. I try to wipe away my tears with the back of my hand as I show him how he can use the machine in English, and when he doesn't take over, I help him through the prompts. He adds the money. I start to tug my suitcase away when a woman halts me.

She wants to go to Slovenia. Slovenia is distinctly *not* in the Vienna city center. I have no clue how to get her to Slovenia with the local trains, surely she needs a regional train, surely she needs someone with more information. She insists. I suggest asking up at the airport information counter. She persists. I have to help; she keeps saying that I have to help.

Finally, another woman arrives and knows how she can get there. The Spaniard—still hanging around—lets me lead him to the proper platform for our mutual train. We've just missed the last one. "What a pity," he says with the glee of being able to say something pithy in a foreign tongue. We wait together, discussing the topics we can manage—his girlfriend, his family, and the beautiful things we've seen in our travels.

I tell him a few stops before our destination, "You know, I was pretty sad when you stopped me."

He laughs, and he gives precisely this reply: "Yes, you were crying. But so! I needed that you helped."

I suppose I needed it as well.

—Vienna

Self-Defense

In Vienna, I terrify a little boy who offers me his seat in the bus. He has a yin-yang patch and an American flag patch affixed his backpack. This makes me smile. When I ask if he does Taekwondo, he thinks I want his bag. Then he seems to think I want the soda in his coat pocket. He tries to offer me whatever he has, as though this is a rather civilized afternoon mugging.

Finally, I reach toward the patch to clarify, and he flinches. He yelps, "I don't speak…"

"Oh," I laugh a bit and apologize. I ask in German if he can speak German.

"No!" Since he answers in English I pause, wanting to mend things. However, when the bus stops, he sprints to the exit. On the sidewalk, he loiters near the stop, hoping to catch the next bus that travels the same route. I realize that I drove him out, and this was my fault—trying to befriend the whole city. Maybe like a good and obedient child he meant, *no, actually, I don't speak to Strangers.*

—Vienna

Rock With You

The bus is running and the doors hang open, but not a single passenger climbs in. At other gates people impatiently crowd the doors, but at #3, everyone waits for an attendant to compel them. Circles of conversation form. Suitcases of various colors and cardboard boxes reinforced with twine are piled just outside the cargo area. No one moves before required. The ride to Pristina will take fifteen hours, after all.

Some men stand in a pack of five with a small boy among them. The boy adopts the posture of his heroes: wrists on their hips, hands behind their backs. They rock on their feet and rush their last cigarettes. The boy waits below the smoke, but directly in the cloud of fumes from the idling bus. He cranes his neck toward the wisecracks traded above.

From a nearby bus or an unseen loudspeaker, the boy perks up at a Michael Jackson song. He spontaneously breaks into a set of moves, right in the center of the group of non-dancers. The men let him be a kid, one man offering him a scatter of applause. The boy tugs down an invisible hat on his head and shoots his other hand up in a skyward point. Almost as quickly, he slides back into the posture of the men, like nothing has happened, still rocking on his feet and twitching happily at the briefly permitted impulse to dance.

—Vienna Südtirolerplatz

Good Health. You're Welcome.

Life can be hard for non-smokers who don't have the tasks and belongings of smokers to keep their hands busy. Instead, we must find ways to wait for buses without hurried drags. I stay occupied by collecting stories.

An old Turkish man arrives to join in the wait. I feel inspired to demonstrate some of the Turkish I've been learning, but not quite confident enough to strike up a conversation. Thankfully, he sneezes. I seize the opportunity and say, in Turkish, "Çok geç!" This is incorrect. I said, "Too late!" instead of "Good health!"

He begins a slow shift toward the speaker, and during the craning of his neck, I try to decide if I'd rather seem like a strange woman talking to herself in Turkish, or as a novice Turkish speaker in Vienna unable to properly wish him well as we wait for the bus. I'm not sure which would be less embarrassing. By the time he faces me, I am bright red, furious with myself for making the error. I offer another try, a penitent: "Çok yaşa?" He nods like a teacher praising the one answer a student might salvage at the end of an exam. These are phrases I should have clear by now, so I'm boiling with self-consciousness. Vain early attempts in a new language are a sure path to humility.

He seems to understand this, so he thanks me easily in his native tongue and turns away. And when he thinks he's moved enough to be out of my view, a full grin is granted across his deeply lined face. He covers his mustache as he gives an exhale of laughter, suppressed to be polite and merciful.

—Vienna

Do-Re-Mi S.O.S.

As the bus merged onto the highway, leaving no chance for unhappy passengers to disembark, a group of Slovakian college students old enough to know better broke into song. The driver remained completely unmoved, plowing on ahead. Somehow believing their entertainment would be appreciated, a boy in a polo shirt led the tune, propping himself against his seat to gaze around at his bold fellows. During his smiling and crooning, craning to catch his compatriots' eyes, he managed to miss the distress of his audience.

Riders scowled and steamed, or scrambled for headphones. A gray-haired lady very near to the conductor's elbow made a great scene of covering her ears with her hands. The songs continued. The mood in the bus sank against the cheer of the choir.

Out the window, a fragile elderly man climbed a ladder to touch up the paint on his elevated shrine for the Virgin Mary. Small religious shrines peppered the villages, but one rarely had a chance to see a restoration in progress. The man extended his brush while clinging to the ladder with the rest of his body.

The grumpy ones glaring out of the bus would have seen him there. Posed in front of a field of sunflowers, he added a bright yellow coat of paint. This slow moving man and his shaky paintbrush became an opportunity for distraction, a gift of peace, for the passengers suffering a ceaseless Slovakian sing-along.

—Bus from Vienna to Bratislava, Slovakia

Oh.

The blonde man wearing a blue shirt struts in immaculate tan shoes. Even behind his sunglasses, I see him light up. Down the sidewalk, a pretty brunette is waving and waving. He crosses the street making a happy diagonal toward her. Though he is swiftly bridging the gap between them, a little boy on a bicycle overtakes him. The boy rides to the gesticulating brunette—a delighted aunt with a singular focus. The little boy was the reason for the happy greetings. He was the one she sought. His mother arrives as well, unsuccessfully dashing after the bike, but greeting the reunion with a small smile.

The blonde man—seeing the scene—cuts a wide curve around and away from the trio. He is blushing and tripping, surely scuffing his shoes. I watch him go, but no one else seems to notice. I'm still wondering: who had he been expecting? Could there be another brunette out there waiting for him? Who did he believe was waving him close?

—Vienna

Smile Like You're Home

Outside the meeting to cover the Dos and Don'ts of volunteering at the asylum seekers center, I feel an urge to dash away. I am always terrified at the thought of something new, an odd daily battle for someone who left her job to live in a foreign country.

The eight-year-old Chechnyan boy has a fauxhawk mullet. We make eye contact before the meeting begins. He looks like my brother. I grin and he hides his face. He's sitting at the table along with three other children.

Another boy wears a New York Yankees cap. "Yankees?" I whisper, "You like baseball?"

He seems surprised: "No."

As the director begins speaking, the Chechnyan boy rests his elbows on the table and clasps his hands like he is praying before a meal. He catches my attention again and giggles silently. He's wearing a black button up shirt with a black four-button vest over it. He cups his hands in front of his mouth and keeps smiling, meeting my eyes, and hiding his grin. I should be listening to the rules, as I'm naturally rule abiding—but as one who is naturally rule abiding, I also feel I'll just know what to do.

The boy blinks at me again and we both laugh at something no one else notices. I forget that I am supposed to be one of the grown-ups. My mind is climbing to gratitude, and how my little brother also has such a spirit and impish grin, and how we had the same home and phone number for our whole lives. How we could stay in one place, and how this boy had to flee, and yet the smile was the same. How we are in ourselves something immovable and portable and resilient.

—Vienna

Nothing to See Here

The little boy sat with his legs folded under him and labored carefully in his notebook, writing plays for Arsenal, his favorite soccer club. A chilly Serbian woman and her boyfriend rested across from the boy, also waiting for a morning flight. As the tiny arms worked, she stared at his labors, enraptured. She became more beautiful. She leaned toward her boyfriend, who put his arm around her. They both slipped into a trance: the boyfriend staring at the TV screen above, the woman focused on the studious boy.

The boy wore a gray and black striped sweater, black corduroy pants, brown loafers. His father stretched out over four nearby seats to sleep. The boy had a red Arsenal pencil bag with a plastic pencil sharpener and ruler, both of which he dropped under the seats, the sharpener skittering away. He had to cross two rows of groggy adults to recover it.

He removed three pencils: yellow, purple, and red, then slowly zipped the bag closed again. He nibbled at his lips as he worked, thumbing through the notebook's pages, most of which had sketches of castles, soccer plays, or the flags of various countries. He read: "A. R. S. Eeeeee. N. Aaaaa. L." Then he tried writing it backward. "L. Aaaa. N. No no no," he turned to another page and stared at the blank sheet to ponder, his forehead in his hand. Then he exhaled–"Phew!"–and flipped through again, talking his way through his work.

On the front of the notebook he had sloppily written his name J-O-E. Then, again JOE underneath more carefully, reflecting pride of his name, the pride of ownership. The Serbian woman's eyes filled with tears, and she turned her smile to her boyfriend. As he gazed down at her expectant face, the boyfriend saw what she saw and began to cough, clear his throat, and grow nervous. He elbowed her and gave a tight smile, then he gestured to his phone and tried to distract her with other, less permanent, features of life.

—Vienna Airport

Personal Space

At mid-morning, the U-Bahn platform was nearly abandoned. The young woman with ceaseless layers walked to her usual waiting place and stopped. From feet to head: boots, legwarmers, long socks, tights, a skirt, a jacket, a sweater, arm warmers, gloves, a scarf, a hat—despite the bundling up, from her shoulders to the ground she made a lean European line.

She glanced at the clock over the platform and smiled. Delighting in the four minutes to wait, she unwound her headphones and set a whimsically serious daydream on her face.

Four tourists buried in a guidebook came down the stairs behind her. They toted closed umbrellas, which doubled as weapons that haplessly impaled bystanders while the visitors huddled over the maps. They moved as a collective group with pale wheat hair, sensible winter walking shoes, glasses down on their noses. Without looking up for a place on the platform, they settled in just next to the girl in her layers.

Snapped from her musical reverie, she eyed them. She moved a bit away, not too abruptly. She just took a small step and a slide to the right, which they seemed instinctively to mirror. They shifted as well, though remaining fixed on the map, the transit plan, the opportunities. Despite the wide-open spaces to wait for the train, they stayed close to her, right behind her. She tugged some of her layers and became impatient, glaring down the track or up at the clock, no longer able to enjoy her platform solitude.

—Vienna

My Carrot-Towel Confusion

He's among a dozen men with stands to sell fruits and vegetables on the Naschmarkt. We've become pals because one day I tried to ask for carrots in Turkish and he laughingly handed me a towel: "Havlu?" I blinked at the towel and pointed to the orange roots nearby. "Havuç," he corrected me and I sighed. He pointed at different veggies and asked me to name them. I failed miserably. He loved every minute of it and sent me away with a free sack of fruit that could have fed a family of five. "I'm only one woman!" I exclaimed, and he laughed again.

This time, he won't let me pay for my strawberries and pears. I keep trying to shove money at him as he walks away. The other men working at the stand watch with hands on their hips my helpless holding out of Euros. "Brother," I tell him in Turkish, "I really thank you, but I am buying this. Now." His colleagues slap their legs and applaud. I scramble together another sentence saying it is very kind, but please! I threaten that I won't come back if I can't pay, and this has the whole staff in near hysterics.

"Go on, girl, go away then." My benefactor wipes tears from his eyes as I hold up the untouched bill. "Next time you pay. Next time," he promises yet again.

—Vienna

Don't Mess With

An anxious Austrian college boy wears a Texas t-shirt, tucked in, and one can see his belt up high on his ribs as he sits in a low café chair. A waiter draws close but walks right by. The boy slips his computer quietly into a much-buckled-and-strapped backpack. He tries not to make any waves, any noise. Wishing to leave, he seems ready to disappear. He adjusts his gadgets and slides his chair back. He tests jingling the zipper of his jacket as he puts it on. Still, the waiter does not pause. The café is nearly empty and the waiter shows no malice, but the boy won't speak up.

The boy unpockets some money, clinking his change, to draw attention, murmuring to himself quietly, then with a bit more volume as the waiter passes. Something weak about "zahlen?" and the waiter nods in his direction, but keeps walking the other way. As the boy shifts, the waiter hustles past again. The boy waits to exist. It seems clear that he could wait like a puddle all day long.

Out of pity, the waiter returns, kind and cheerful. For the first time, one can see they are both boys, both the same age. The waiter counts his change, slaps the anxious boy on the shoulder in friendship. The waiter offers sage advice (in German), "Next time, say something!" The boy—very clearly not from Texas—smiles at the slap, receives the acknowledgment, zips his bag and hurries to the tram under his freshly-earned command of the universe.

—Vienna

I Spy

A couple and their toddler toddle through the hip Vienna neighborhood. As they come into an area with shops, cafes, and restaurants, the father lifts the tiny girl up onto his shoulders. She sits with her knees on his clavicle, her hands on top of his head. She rides proudly atop her father's height. Her curls bounce as he steps. She moves her head happily to a song no one else can hear.

She turns left and notices a child in the windows of a clothing store. It is her reflection—moving from one window to the next, high above her usual perspective. She moves in a slight jolt until she finally makes the connection. She watches herself in the glass, but has noticed that walls or doors cast no reflection. So she gazes at the buildings on her side, looking ahead during the wall sections, looking at herself in the windows as mirrors when her family passes. Back and forth, she can view the street and then herself. She plays the game of glancing for about two blocks, then noting the last windowpane before a crosswalk, she turns to herself and waves goodbye.

—Vienna

Take Care

The bus trip from Vienna to Trogir, Croatia takes twelve hours and rolls overnight. As the monster idles—half the passengers taking final drags on cigarettes or patting at their relatives—a mother helps her teenaged son to his seat. The mother gazes around the bus that would carry her boy away. He walks her back out, embraces and kisses her, then boards calmly and settles in.

She waits on the platform, requiring confirmation that the trip was underway before she would go home. Her son makes kind gestures to his worried mother outside. The bus is so tall, the windows so high, that she looks up at her son like he is a cat trapped in a tree. The departure is three minutes behind schedule already—a sign it is not an Austrian bus line. In those three minutes, she switches between studying her watch and convincing herself not to board again for one more hug, for one last word of advice. She shivers into her coat.

Her son stands so she can see him more clearly and makes motions that she should leave, that she should go, that she must be cold. She waves them off with her hand, then her head. Even as the bus pulls away, they keep their eyes on each other, even as he cranes around completely in his seat and she rushes to another platform to catch the last view of his shadow against the window.

The bus circles the station and drives the perimeter of the parking lot before arriving at the proper exit, and his mother still waits to wave once more as the bus passes her in the street.

They are the only two people on the bus, in the station, in that ridiculously beautiful few minutes. Perhaps this is one reason people have children. Someone to miss, someone to worry over, someone to wave back.

—Vienna

Stories from Elsewhere in Europe

For Harisa

Five years ago, I met a beautiful woman from Bosnia on a flight. We had spotted each other before we boarded, and since the plane wasn't totally full, she came over to sit near me. We talked the whole time about books and life. We laughed like old friends.

She was kind and warm. She immediately invited me to visit her family–to ditch my present vacation and join her. I loved that, though I had to decline. We kept in touch from time to time and she encouraged me to keep writing.

It's remarkable how someone I met for only a few hours made me brave for adventure, hopeful about the future, and helped me to discover that love is a bigger part of the world than any other element. She gave this to me.

When I learned she had passed away suddenly, my heart broke for her husband and her son, for her family, for her colleagues and friends. I really only spoke with her for a few hours, but she became such an important part of my journey. She is a reminder that no encounter is just a drop in the bucket, but that they can all matter.

A note I sent to Harisa from 2012:

"I ran across you in my travel notes. I guess I saw you even before we got in the flight. I didn't write quite enough about you to create a whole story, but I somehow knew you were an extraordinary person."

With gratitude for her kindness and openness, and with sympathy for her family.

-Paige

Groove, Death, Italians

"Groove is in the Heart" is on the radio, and the Italian tourists are certain that we're all going to die. For me, the pace and aggressive passing of Croatian bus drivers was no longer alarming. I've been on this route many times. I hope I'm not losing my gratitude as we fly down the coastal road, but I've lost that panicky thought that these will be my final moments.

Back at Makarska, the driver sat for a coffee with a remarkable sense of self. He winked at me and smoothed his hair. He flirted with the sixty-year-old waitress. So I don't clutch at the handles of the seats when we pass the lumber truck, when we pass the wagon and trailer. I don't look nervously at the guardrail and consider how insufficient it would be to stop a fast-moving bus. I trust him to preserve himself first, and the rest of us because we happen to be seated behind him. He drives this all day, nearly every day, so it is best to rely on his broad self-protection and his well-worn habits.

—On the bus from Split to Medjugorje, Bosnia-Herzegovina

Achtung: Puderzucker

A man at a crosswalk unsheathes a freshly purchased chocolate croissant. He is exceedingly tall, boyish in his impatience, but adult enough to be wary of the powdered sugar on top of his snack. He eyes his black suit coat, then holds the pastry to his right side and begins to huff and puff. He blows the sugar into the wind before taking a bite. Unbeknownst to a man so tall, a small woman with white hair approaches and stands next to him, along with so many others obediently waiting for walking to be permitted. He finds more potentially disgraceful sugar, and he blows it off with one full, loud exhale—dusting the sugar over his shocked little neighbor. She gazes up into the cloud, and he gazes down from it—in a moment ripped from slapstick comedy and scattered all over the sidewalk.

—Munich, Germany

The Shared Eyebrow and the Runaway Tablet

He is in a blue jogging suit and winter coat, she wears leggings as pants with a ski jacket. They stand close while waiting for the plane. She tries to hand him his ticket and passport, but he pushes them back. She is to be in charge. The woman has overly plucked eyebrows that she penciled in with a dark line almost to her temple. Her boyfriend has one thick unibrow, which makes a person suddenly remember songs from Ernie and Bert on Sesame Street. With she too few and he too many, they remain shockingly inexpressive. Yet, he pulls her close for a hug, and she keeps her head slightly tilted to avoid smudging her pretend eyebrows on the shoulder of his jacket.

During the flight, they remain in close contact, leaning heads on the other's shoulder, trading knowing glances: A perfect pair.

Upon landing, the woman in the row behind them, who keeps company onboard only with her tablet computer, loses her sole companion. The gadget slips from her hands. Her squeal makes the shared eyebrow rise.

The couple could intervene, could snatch the device where it falls at their feet, if they hadn't been holding hands. Their brows turn toward the dropped object, but their reaction time is slowed by affection. So their neighbor's tablet, with its sleek design, slides like a hockey puck down the center aisle as the airplane angles down for landing.

Passengers in aisle seats gasp in fright as it passes, thinking a woodland creature is scurrying by. The plane arranges itself for the runway and edges right a bit, so the tablet finally slides to a stop at the feet of passengers in 7 D, E, and F. The shared brow couple sniffs, not undone by their lack of action. They have their priorities straight and their fingers entwined.

—Flight from Budapest, Hungary to London Heathrow

Random Apple of Kindness

Our checkout woman has short, funky blonde hair and she's been very unhappily scanning groceries for a ceaseless line of customers. I don't blame her for being grumpy.

I'm with my dear friend Nora, a beautiful, compassionate Hungarian woman with whom I regularly melt into laughter. During my visit, I busy her with various translation tasks, such as my present request, "Can you ask her for a little plastic bag since the Túró is getting everywhere?" My favorite dairy product is leaving a spot on the conveyor belt.

The clerk scans and we hustle to sack up my items. I'm collecting envelopes of mulled wine spices and preparing not to understand the total when the clerk will say it aloud. I've had no luck in Hungarian, and most of my attempts make Nora say, "Awww," with kindness before she breaks out in giggles. The last of my selections is equally pathetic—a single apple. While in line, I had pointed out that it was the only produce among my purchases.

I have done something wrong. This is clear. The checkout woman is glaring at my apple as she picks it up. It isn't computing for me that I forgot to use the machine in produce to weigh and label my foray into fresh fruit, as is the custom in this particular market. Even as she sneers, I still don't understand what I've done. I wonder if she sees a flaw in the apple, perhaps a bruise I might have missed.

In a flash, the clerk turns away and chucks my unbought apple, skeeball-style, up the conveyor belt of the empty checkout lane behind her. She turns back to face me and mutters my total.

It feels surreal as I watch my attempt at Golden Delicious rolling away, but I offer my payment as the next customers shuffle closer. I slowly move on, but not before the lady behind me in line gets my attention. She hands me an apple.

I'm holding the fruit, wondering if I'd had some sort of episode. Nora asks, "Did they give that to you?"

I'm in a daze of hustled grocery stuffing and words I couldn't understand, so we watch the apple-deliverer her companion paying for their properly-labeled produce. They also stood in the line to get what they needed, just a few things for such a long wait, and yet it seems they have given me an apple from their purchases.

It takes me forever to realize what has happened. I'm so accustomed to traveling alone and watching everything around me, but in the store I had been wrapped up with my friend. With her I could be shy, overwhelmed, and not very observant. Even now, the kindness of the apple-deliverer makes me want to cry. She saw me through my distraction. She confirmed that it was indeed their random apple of kindness, and I felt relieved that I could have Nora there to translate this gratitude. While I stood next to Nora nodding, grinning, and trying my mispronounced Hungarian "thank you," I hope we managed to convey our delight at their watchful, thoughtful generosity.

—Budapest, Hungary

The Impatient Italians and the Fighting Irish

In Medjugorje, there's a crowd of people entering the church, praying at the grotto, climbing steep hills in prayer. It's a place of retreat, usually quiet, usually peaceful.

This morning there's a long queue at the ladies' room between Masses. Waiting in the line are speakers of many languages, but two Italian women walk right past us, ignoring the single-file suckers. They march to the front and go for the next doors that open.

Two Irish women are supposed to be next and also head toward those recently vacated stalls. One of them is younger, the other older and determined. The older steps in front of the women who cut ahead, and forces her way into the stall that is rightfully hers. The Italian women begin to scream, raise their hands, make a scene–almost precisely as the church bells ring outside. Women in line tsk-tsk, and the lady next to me says, "Italians! They never think the rules apply to them!" I don't have enough evidence to weigh in. Though I have met several seemingly nice Italians on this trip, I have noticed many were often maneuvering ahead of me in lines.

The younger Irish woman exits her stall first and hustles past the Italian women. She glances at those of us in line with a blush. The Waiting Women nod at her with encouragement and support. The older woman takes a slower approach, her head held high, knowing she did the right thing.

I catch up with the Irish women outside, feeling I must ask about their encounter. The older one laughs, "I don't know how I turned into a fish man's wife! I've been here on pilgrimage for a week, and I felt so much peace. But I just couldn't let them cut the queue." There's a rosy glow to her cheeks, and she seems enlivened to have stood up for all the Waiting Women.

The younger also smiles at compelling order on those who tried to cut ahead. "There's a reason people wait in line. It's only right. Especially here!" It is a marvel that anyone could be rude at a pilgrimage site, and to two women so kind and dear.

"So now," the older woman grins at me and leans in close, "So now you've really seen the Fighting Irish."

—Medjugorje, Bosnia-Herzegovina

A Love Story in Eight Bus Stops

This is perhaps the only time in recorded history when a woman has given a double-take to a man in a beige running suit and fanny pack.

He boards the bus and she catches him right away. Between glances, his scruffy neck flushes red as he blinks out of the graffiti-covered window. Then he notices that she saw what he had seen—a spark in someone else, a moment worthy of a second glance—and he becomes more confident, more curious. He meets her gaze and holds it.

The two locked in the stare are probably strangers. She stands in a group of potential suitors, one guy standing close enough to have required some permission. This fickle dude had been leering at another girl's legs until he discovered the woman was looking away. Now he reaches his arm across a rail between the electric gaze, but she just straightens her neck and stares at the young man in the running suit.

Around them, people shout and sigh, as these two create suspense in a tedious afternoon. He begins to shift and adjust his gold necklace, which the woman in her fashion patience also forgives. His gathered brow adds detail to his look, adds helplessness as he rings for his stop.

He stands and she shifts her jaw. He moves close to pass her but still heads for the exit. They whisper the local goodbye. She watches him leave through the closing doors, through the pedestrians he joins, and she disappears into a smile. Lost to all the other passengers merely moving from one place to another, she discovers something remote.

She should have followed him out, perhaps, or he should have taken a detour. Still, it was nice to admire what they did have instead: four minutes on a bus in a long contented glance. Boldness may have made a better film, but some love stories are more beautiful abridged.

—Novi Sad, Serbia

Waiting for Eve

The mix of humanity at the Budapest bus stop included backpackers, Spaniards, grandmothers with grandchildren, and the Miss Eden Contestants of 2011.

Several of the teenage girls stood by pink rolling suitcases. Nearly all were clenching their hands or tugging at their clothing. As new competitors arrived, each received stares and hair flips and thin smiles, all mannerisms stolen from the movies and executed with a lack of skill. One girl broke the facade completely and exhaled while looking sadly up at the clouds.

A guy with hipster glasses and Converse shoes kept a cell phone at his ear and a strained look on his face. It was his job to gather the girls and half-embrace them as he put on their sashes. He took pains to make it appear painful. Their private bus slowed and parked behind an idling discount line to Prague, whose ticket-holders slowly realized they would not be traveling with Beauty that day.

There were only two sashes left to distribute as a tall brunette approached, walking ahead of her industrial-strength father and zebra-print suitcase. Eyeing Hipster as he sashed his daughter, Big Dad took her aside for and a paternal pat on the shoulder. There was one more sash; there must be one more girl and hence no hurry.

However, the other bus was scheduled to depart. So the less-polished riders hesitantly began to board. Those in the far right seats kept looking out, waiting for the last more-than-fashionably-late contestant to arrive.

She still had not appeared as the bus to Prague rolled away. There wasn't an audible groan, but a collective rustle of passengers pretending that they weren't all that interested anyway, as they turned quickly to their newspapers, their armrests, their settling in.

—Budapest, Hungary

Something So Perfect

It's my first trip to Europe. I'm 27. I'm in Vienna's Albertina Museum. I'm trying to pay attention to Picasso's distorted ladies and bullfighters. Instead, I keep getting distracted by a handsome guy carrying a sizable novel. The cover is printed in a language peppered with accent marks. Though we make eye contact often and smile, I am still in a state of anxiety that marks my first days abroad. I do wonder if he may be planning to mug me, even as he gives me shy glances through the exhibit. I'm trying to be like people in movies who go to Europe and find themselves, who never seem plagued by memories of being in junior high or worries about petty crime.

We depart at about the same moment—I with Eric, my dear friend who promised me I would fall in love with Europe, and the book man with a grandmotherly figure. We stand so close at one moment that we almost speak, then we don't. As we leave, I take a picture of the narrow Vienna street he is treading in order to catch his departing profile. I spend the rest of the day smiling to myself in amazement at having been seen.

Eric and I roam for another day in Vienna then take a bus to Prague, where Eric is living. I'll be on my own during the days and will have to conquer my nervousness by heading out solo. Jan—a lovely local friend of mine—tells me which buses to take and avoid. He advises me not to rush for the subway since the trains will be frequent.

So one day, I endeavor a long escalator down to a metro station. A train is arriving, and I know I won't make it, so I stop and pretend to read an advertisement. People rush out of the train. Someone crashes into me head on. *Sorry!* My English apology comes first, as he says what must have been *Sorry* in Czech—though I'd been saying that word all day as *Hello*.

After the shock of the collision, we recognize each other for a blink. We start off in our opposite directions, and then we both stop. It's like a yogurt commercial.

Even without the giant book, I know he's the man from the museum. He walks back toward me and we stand in amazement. His name is Lukas; he studied English in New Jersey. He's holding a newspaper. He asks how I'm enjoying Prague.

Four days and a country away, we marvel at the chance to meet. This is enough. We say our hellos and our goodbyes in the same two minutes. He tells me to enjoy my stay and I promise I will, then he takes the steep escalator up to the street. Even with the nervousness and newness, it does seem I am falling in love with Europe. I take the next metro train without rushing, grinning and delighted to have discovered something so perfect.

—Vienna and Prague

Resolution

"Beware of pickpocketers while praying." I pass the sign in the entryway to the Church of the Infant of Prague. I keep my hands in my empty pockets. I admire the saints admiring the sky and watch my breath rising. The pine scent from the Christmas trees is fantastic and competes with the chill of the building and the breeze of the street—the doors constantly propped open by slow-moving troupes of tourists.

As I stand near a statue of a saint I don't know, a monk approaches. His brown robe rustles and I move out of his way, my typical posture of trying to be polite and unobtrusive. He's looking at me, so I turn and smile. His eyes are deep-set and blue, his eyebrows a salt-and-pepper hedge.

"Where are you from?" He asks, but it's not really a question, I suspect, because as I say the United States and he's ready with a follow-up: "Can you name all Fifty?"

For half a guilty second I wonder if I'm being called upon for fifty saints or fifty prayers, "Oh. The States? Hmmm. Maybe forty?"

"Not bad." He gestures at me, so I nod and genuflect as a reaction. I promise myself to brush up on all of it next year, those small East Coast states and the major statue-able saints.

—Prague, Czech Republic

Respect

I get to sit by him! The little old Japanese man I spotted back in the glacial airport check-in lines–he's in my row and he will be spied upon.

He wears a surgical mask, sits for a while with his feet tucked under his thighs. He peers out of thick glasses. He has wispy hair and vine-like eyebrows. The classic Grandpa cardigan keeps him warm.

His wife rests in the seat between us, so short her feet only touch the floor when she points them. My bag is under the seat in front of me and when I lean to get a pen, she thinks I am bowing. She bows lower. I bow back.

Later I need lip balm, a snack, another book—any time I reach for my bag she begins to bow. We set off a series of respectful awkwardness in the small space above the seat pocket. I want to say something—thank you or a correlative, respectful term for a cease-fire—but suddenly the only Japanese that comes to mind is, "Domo Arigato, Mr. Roboto," and I have no idea what that means either.

So we just keep smiling and bowing. The little old man by the window sometimes watches the contest, sometimes skims a Japanese guidebook about Budapest, and sometimes stares straight ahead, his eyes are not drooping closed with exhaustion. Not yet. Not on their first leg.

When we arrive, there is an echo of clicks from unlatched seatbelts as the announcement asks people to stay seated during taxi. It's not an emergency evacuation, but a moment of contagious restlessness. People stand and start pushing forward. We are only going to a shuttle bus on the ground, after all. Once out of the plane, the waiting will continue, but there was no desire on the part of the passengers to let rows in front of them depart first.

Channeling someone much tougher than myself, I move into the aisle and hold back the maddening crowd so my darling and miniature seat-mates can climb out of the airplane before being overrun. I quite enjoy compelling politeness out of the 30+ numbered rows. As they grumble, I smile. And when I enter the shuttle, my seatmates offer me one last excellent bow. So we are even.

—Flight from Budapest to London

On The (This Isn't A) Road

Trying to get back to the chapel, I find a sign that points vaguely at two different roads. Perhaps it's Robert Frost's eyebrow-raise that points me to the red rocky one.

I go down a hill and start to cross a path of stones, but they don't fit together, each step sways beneath me.

After about twenty careful paces, with a quarter of a mile still to cross, I realize I am not on anything that could resemble a road. I am on a rock pile and that is that. The stack of stones was set there perhaps for some purpose, but not for crossing. My foot slides between two hard places and I get frustrated with myself. This could get treacherous. And it feels hot all of a sudden. And I am probably trespassing. Also, there are probably snakes.

Trespassing AND snakes. So I break into a run. I sprint to reach the end of the long stretch of wobbling rocks. I keep laughing at myself as I rush, tumbling forward without grace, hopefully unseen.

I think of a day from my childhood. From our household of seven, we had a bag of unmatched socks in the laundry room. They waited in vain for a companion to be unearthed. One winter, after a snowfall, I put on several layers of random unpaired socks and ran across the snow without shoes. I wanted to see what it was like to race against the elements. I wanted to see how far I could go before I felt the cold.

This is also a tendency of mine—to wish to run when I should walk, to grow impatient as life is revealed to me, to insist I must speak the language when I've only begun to learn it, to want to cross the threshold and evade notice at the same time. To hike the two pilgrimage hills where the stones are slick and sharp, where the tourists walk devoutly, where the path is rugged but clear. Then I would seek a different, absurd, unoccupied path and decide that this is the one I must take.

—Medjugorje, Bosnia-Herzegovina

Carpe Diem, Handsome Farmer

He had been handsome when younger. He remained handsome but had reached an age where people gazed at him like his days were numbered. He shuffled down the narrow hallway with a small green pepper and two tomatoes in his hand. He could see the Hungarian woman's legs through the glass door of her train compartment. During his double-take, he ran into the door at the end of the hallway like something out of a silent film.

On his return from washing the produce, he passed slowly, aiming to catch a glance at her face, but she remained cloaked behind a newspaper. He paused right outside the door. Waiting a bit with his eyes on the statesman gracing the front page, just above the fold, just where her eyes moved across an article on the other side. He considered the occupants surrounding the woman's legs: an antique Japanese man eating a pear from the top down—core and all, a woman his own age with her hands folded in her lap, and an average looking twenty-something with headphones on.

Feeling bold and immortal, he stepped inside the compartment. The Japanese man nibbled at his pear, the older woman fished for her ticket since she thought this was his reason to enter, and the headphones gave safe cover to the girl looking out the window. The man tried a Serbian greeting at the newspaper to no avail. Then he tried German. The newspaper was drawn down slowly, and the Hungarian woman gazed up, unflappable, before she replied to his greetings in her native tongue. Faced with such a wordless opportunity, the man opted to place one hand over his heart, bat his eyelashes, and hold out his nicely rinsed vegetables for her consideration. She let there be some drama in her indecision, before she selected a tomato, offered a smile of gratitude, and lifted her newspaper again.

The man stumbled from the compartment, overjoyed. He paced by the door several other times before they reached their destination, only to find the woman above those legs still reading the same newspaper, still smirking behind it, a tomato untouched on the seat beside her.

—Train from Belgrade to Budapest

Neighborly

The eleven-year-old girl on the bus moves over to sit in front of her mother. This way she is now in the row across the aisle from me, so we can see each other. She gives me a tight-lipped, shy smile, and I return it. As we ride along, she slumps and points her toes in order to touch the floor. She unzips the front pocket of her book bag and dips her fingers into a trove of pens and pencils. She feels at them, then leaves her fingers there, as though the writing utensils are holding her hand. She sighs and closes her eyes.

Later, she studies me. She peers over. She seems to wonder what I see out the window that makes me stare past her, over her head, then smile to myself and scrawl in my notebook, remarkably steady in our swaying bus. I note small plowed fields, hand-planted with beans, but seemingly no houses nearby. I note the light before sunset making the young greenery glow. She doesn't see these things. The girl sits up straight to mimic my posture and smirk.

I can't help but show how exciting and beautiful I find it to be. I'm pleased to be here and I won't wipe it off my face, even though this makes me a particular oddity. Her mother speaks with me, quietly, asking where I'm from and saying it's odd to have visitors here in March. The girl says something to her mother that I can't understand, and they both smile at me like tourists themselves. "Enjoy your stay," the mother says as they depart, the young girl nodding her goodbye. And they wave from the road as the bus pulls away.

—Herceg Novi, Montenegro

Carry On

Several members of the Hajduk Split soccer team coalesced outside the airplane. Since the players were fit, many were the first out. They wore matching tracksuits. A few punched at each other, a few wandered toward the terminal in meditation over their cell phones. Eventually a different group of players appeared, also in uniforms, following a handful of antique nuns in black habits moving down the stairs to the tarmac. They were followed by the last of the players who helped to carry the baggage for the Sisters. These boys chatted easily with the nuns, as the groups made each other laugh. Passengers in vacation uniforms and business suit uniforms began to disembark without the same team reception.

This scene went unnoticed by most people waiting at the gate above, including two tall, beautiful sisters bearing Croatian passports and a small girl. The girl toted a speckled, stuffed dog and puffed out her cheeks as the supermodel-most-likely-to-be-her-mother began to adjust her the little girl's braid.

In the next moment, the girl whipped her head to the side, causing the release of her hair and the unraveling of her mother's handiwork. A new plane came in for a landing outside. Before the mother could scold her, the girl squealed with delight. Other passengers snapped from their stares of waiting. The girl called out happily about her upcoming flight; she tossed her dog in the air and caught it. She hugged her toy fiercely, found this wasn't sufficient, then pounced on her mother for a hug that could be returned. The woman adjusted her jewelry and laughed quietly, letting this carry on for a moment, before turning her daughter around and resuming work on the braid. The women exchanged a look over the girl's head, a smile that didn't permit such outbursts, but revealed pleasure at a reminder of the joy of flight.

—Split Airport, Croatia

To Pass the Time

Among the many reasons I like Croatian bus drivers is that they will carry on conversations with you knowing full well you don't speak the language. A test of your sense of humor, perhaps. A display of their own. A smile and a slow blink seems to demonstrate the proper respect and good spirit.

Our bus stopped at the border crossing and when the engine cut, it became clear from the sigh of our driver that the wait would be long and August hot. He crawled out with our stack of passports and disappeared into an office.

In the backseat of a car idling in another line, a little girl leaned close to her window. She craned her neck to gaze at our massive bus. She mimed eating corn on the cob while rolling her eyes and wagging her head. Adorable, she chattered away, entertaining herself while her parents offered identification to the guards. She finished one invisible cob and started on another until she collapsed into a fit of laughter. This drew glances from her parents—her father using the rearview mirror, her mother shifting in the passenger seat. The little girl only laughed harder under their gaze, causing her parents to crack smiles as well.

—Border Crossing: Croatia into Montenegro

The Photog's Fury

The bus began its journey thanks to several male passengers who got out to push the slow rolling mass out of its parking stall. After that, things went fairly smoothly.

The drive around the Bay of Kotor is a wonder: water resting under the mountains like a mirage. A Russian woman tries and fails to take photos as the bus rounds the canyon.

In the hot weather, people jump from cement piers that line the road, diving into water that would not rank among the world's clearest, but which had its features of note, like the shadows from churches where monks used to hide.

At no point does the woman stop looking through her camera. She doesn't give up and stare at the water itself, which is tranquil, which won't be hard to recall with fondness. Rather, she wants a record. Her insistence on taking it home makes the water nervous, elusive, stubborn. The camera clicks. She clicks her tongue. She snaps seven, eight photos, then skims through them, groaning quietly, trying again. In most of the pictures, she captures her hazy self scowling into the camera, reflecting in the dust-caked bus window. Sometimes the water seems to break through, but usually alongside a blinding glare of the sun against the glass.

Determined not to forget, she snaps and clicks, remarkably hopeful, ceaseless, as though the very next shot will be the final thing that she had been waiting to preserve.

—Near Kotor, Montenegro

Shoulder to Shoulder

On the winding road down the Croatian coast, a couple gazes toward the turquoise sea, which so beautiful that one usually only sees it in movies. She exhales, "We're driving in the clouds." But he grumbles: "It's just a high fog, you know." She exhales again.

Under the rosary that hung from the rearview mirror and no-smoking sticker mandated by the bus line, the driver expertly lights a cigarette. Nobody moves, except to blink in their nicotine envy.

An antique woman flags down the bus. She climbs the stairs quickly, then returns to feeble as she stares down a tourist occupying the front seat. The tourist hoists his backpack onto his lap to make room, then tries to read his guidebook under a pile of gear. The old woman makes loud small talk with the driver for about five minutes, then he drops her off where she points, though it seems the middle of nowhere. She pats the driver's shoulder and casts a long glare at the tourist before departing into a field.

The driver stops to fuel up. He puts on a little plastic glove to pump the gas, absurd fastidiousness for the burly road wrangler. At a border crossing, he paces impatiently. The passengers inside look out at his ceaseless cigarettes and make small moans. As the time drags on he kicks his own tires. Eventually, the guards in their powder blue polyester coats hand over the stack of his passengers' passports and he leaps into the bus, hoisting the pile at the wayward tourist. "Give." He points to the rear of the bus, fires up the engine, drives onward. The tourist takes his duty very seriously, very slowly, glancing through each passport to find his own, then attempting to identify his fellow travelers by their photos.

Days seem to pass before someone intervenes. A man in sunglasses, several gold chains, and a matching running suit stands and seizes the documents. He gazes out at the crowd—over his painstakingly-tended chest hair—and starts reading the names aloud. Owners raise their hands politely. He has little trouble with the local names, spots a German girl without trouble, but laughs out loud before hunting for: "Suzuki? Suzuki?"

When Suzuki extends his arm and claims his passport, the golden volunteer pats the visitor firmly on his shoulder. Tourists note this as a gesture they might try later, if necessary, to make inroads on such curved journeys.

—Somewhere between Split, Croatia and Budva, Montenegro

The Symphony: Part I

In the lobby, I spot him first. His gray hair is neatly tended. He wears a green tweed sports coat and a tie with small printed horses. I notice his contrasting pocket square. It must be nice to have a symphony date who wears a pocket square. When he passes I smile at him. He seems like someone I might meet one day–when I am living in a nursing home, when I may finally be prepared to settle down.

His wife wears a peach scarf and thick glasses. She moves by him and reaches for his elbow, which is tucked closely to his side. She stops herself. Later she tries again as a sort of reflexive habit, but she stops herself again, not quite daring to touch his sleeve.

I notice as we wait that I may have misjudged the duration of their relationship. Neither of them wears a ring. They move close and then apart. They seem enthralled by what the other says. I start to think this is early flirting. They are part of a tour group of retirees who take up two long rows in the concert hall. Their cluster is uniformly happy and free. Perhaps this is what it is to be finished with work—to take a tour, going to the symphony in a slow-moving herd, packing one nice outfit in your suitcase. As everyone shuffles to their seats, these two sit side-by-side. Though I thought they were fixed, I begin to hope the couple has just met. And, in any case I wish them a lovely beginning.

—Krakow, Poland

The Symphony: Part II

A little girl of about eight years old is a few seats to my left, but she isn't seated. She stands through the whole first movement, wearing a red velvet dress with long sleeves and a white collar. I can feel the little girl watching me as I watch the performance—so I aim to appear very intent. Many others have settled in to listen, slumped down with heads back, eyes closed. When the music gets suddenly loud, you see a wave of jolts from people who have fallen asleep—a leg kicks out, a head snaps upright. I feel my neighbor girl's eyes looking to the stage, then over at me, so I keep smiling, keep trying to demonstrate that I am enjoying the music.

During intermission, I take out my notebook to write and the little girl tries to read what I'm scrawling, despite the distance and language barrier. I notice we're wearing the same flat shoes–mine are blue and hers are red. So I cross one leg and shake my foot. She watches my ankle, then lights up and gazes down to her own feet. We raise our eyebrows conspiratorially. We could certainly exit the concert hall far more swiftly than the ladies wearing high heels.

As the music resumes, it's clear the girl must be familiar with the selection. She's trying hard to keep herself from conducting, sometimes she can't restrain her joy and must reach out, must set the tempo, must release a section with her hand. Her father tries not to inhibit her, but whispers from time to time. She's giddy, so I wish to be giddy. She lets out a loud sigh, then covers her mouth, then turns her eyes toward me, and I return her glance with a nod of respect. It's become a totally different experience than I had expected, and a joy to listen to the music under her contagious glee.

—Krakow, Poland

Upbringing

A family of four walks through the falling leaves as they circle the castle. Dad has a camera with an extensive telephoto lens. One son walks, hops, stomps alongside the others. His mother pushes the younger son in a stroller. Mom slows alongside a row of parked cars, "Antonio," she calls.

The child in the stroller sits up at the sound of his name. He turns to his mother, then cranes his neck back in the direction where Mom is nodding. He takes in a shiny black sedan.

"Mercedes," he recites.

"Bravo!" Mom is pleased.

The boy in the stroller looks to the next car, an SUV-truck of sorts, raised on large tires, with a bar added on for lights above the windshield, a rope for towing. "Mama?"

"Eh. Mitsubishi," Mom is unimpressed, but the boy keeps studying the vehicle as they pass. The son on foot skips on ahead, Dad walks behind. And Mom hustles the family past a Toyota without comment.

—Krakow, Poland

Wandering and Mispronunciation

A friend asked me, "What did you do in Krakow?" I smiled to myself because my chief activity was wandering. I walked for hours in random directions. I sat in parks to people watch. I saw a boy kicking leaves like an endless supply of soccer balls, lost in his own game, complete with sound effects. I spotted a young woman who also watched the boy and delighted at his happy solitude. She walked away wearing a broad, reflective smile with her hands deep in the pockets of her pale blue coat. Near my apartment, and through each neighborhood, I watched little oldsters go out on their balconies and lean. They leaned over the city, over their courtyard, over their pots of flowers or air-drying laundry.

My second hobby was church hopping. There are ceaseless Catholic churches in Krakow, so it was a delight to go from one to the next. I would exit, look left or right, and head for the next steeple. In one small chapel, a nun handed me five plastic medals, gestured to the icon of Mary and Jesus, and began to whisper a story. Random patches of the Croatian language were coming to me. I had been passing off the Croatian "goodbye" all week, though the Polish goodbye has a different pronunciation. I tried to say I didn't understand, hoping it was a cognate to Polish: "Ne razumijem." She nodded happily and tried to tell me her tale again, but with a bit more volume. I kept shrugging and putting my hand over my chest in apology as she kept on chatting and smiling. Finally, I started to laugh almost silently, and she joined in.

It was a perfect, quiet, peaceful week full of surprising October sunshine. Next time, I'll sigh off my balcony, learn a few more phrases, try to find the nun, and aim to translate my gratitude.

—Post-Krakow, Poland

The Wave

The family of three heads for seats in the tram. The mother has a toy for her toddler, who refuses to remain in one place. The father tries to wrangle his boy and distract him with things out the window. The Dad points, the boy glances, and since I happen to be standing on the sidewalk near their windows, I wave hello.

The little boy breaks into a grin, and I reply in kind. He moves close to the window to watch me. His mother takes his wrist and jiggles his arm to mimic my movement. The father is nodding, glowing, happy to watch this unfold. Then their suddenly-independent boy pulls his arm away from his dear, now-laughing mother. He stretches his hand wide and waves at me all by himself.

—Sarajevo, Bosnia-Herzegovina

Next Stop

As usual, stops were not announced on the train. People familiar with the route rushed the hallways as we pulled into a station—or the last scraps of one. The train paused, the people fled, and the machine continued. Ages before a vague arrival time, I grew terrified that I would miss my stop. I suffered this particular anxiety on every trip. It became a typical part of what I carried on.

A woman and I shared legroom in our train compartment. We kept accidentally kicking and stomping each other but stopped making polite apology smiles somewhere around hour two. Since this woman was able to engage in small talk with the passport control boy, I waited until he left and asked if she knew which stop might be Novi Sad. She blinked, pressed down a smile. This was also her destination and she pledged to take me along. So finally, rather than reading a paragraph in my book, staring anxiously out the window, re-reading the paragraph, and checking my watch–finally, I could make some progress.

Later, she stood, gave me a nod, and we moved into the snug train hallway for our unannounced arrival. She was blonde and fair, single, an only child, an online trader in Budapest waiting for her big break so she could leave Europe and "chase that rainbow." She smiled to herself, even as I stood right next to her. From the slow-rolling train, she directed my attention to her childhood home just outside of the city, and as we approached the center she pointed to her parents' new flat. She asked about the thick novel I was reading and I asked about her similarly sizable book. We spoke vaguely about authors, trains, ambitions.

As we edged toward the exit, she asked what had been on her mind since hour two. She wanted to know why an American was going to Novi Sad. And I smiled to myself, even as she stood right next to me. How could I explain?

—Train from Budapest, Hungary, to Novi Sad, Serbia

Novi Sad: Part I

Most of the girls in town have long, straight-cut bangs that make a horizon over their eyebrows. Most of the girls hold cigarettes in their unsmiling mouths. They pout as advertisements have taught them. But this girl has wavy hair, and while she has mastered that same serious look, it is clear that she is more than the pose. She is lean and watchful, with eyes that notify you if you're being seen. She blinks and you know it. She hangs out with a group of three boys, content to be a part of the team. And she clearly can't wait to be friendly, but will stay patient until she becomes acquainted with me, with this visitor. As she gets ready for the evening, she plans to iron a pair of loose brown pants.

They chat in Serbian, the twenty-somethings that are my hosts. Yet, they try not leave me out. They make an effort to smile in my direction. They devise a plan to show off their town. When I blink back at the girl, she finally offers a relieved, stunning smile.

She discovers the iron won't work. Two of her friends take it apart, then tinker with the inside, fix the screws tighter. She plugs it in and smoke puffs out. After a pause, nothing more happens, so the taller boy shakes the iron and helps with the task by holding out the pant legs while she flattens them.

On the bus ride to our first outing, the watchful girl offers me a few translations. She says that people around us are all talking about money. Even those who had been on vacations, who had the good fortune to go abroad, are only talking about what was expensive or what was cheap. Not about the people they met or times they had. She said it was okay that I didn't understand. Instead, she and her friends dream about where they would go if they were to take a vacation. South East Asia, they mention, but there is a consensus on Hawaii. Their parents all wanted to go to Hawaii, and so do they. Hawaii. They gaze out the windows until our stop.

—Novi Sad, Serbia

Novi Sad: Part II

My hosts take me to the hill by the Clock Tower. We pause. They confer and the beautiful girl sighs at them, then asks me if I would mind drinking from the same bottle of beer. They always did, they didn't know where to find cups. *Nema problema*, I assure them that I also want to be a part of the usual routine. The boys applaud. I want to contribute, but they shake their heads. "You are our guest."

We climb up slowly. They grow quiet as the sun sets. The city lights up. To avoid melancholy, someone begins a series of jokes in Serbian. I catch the name "Chuck Norris," pleasantly surprised to hear him as an international joke protagonist. As they explode in laughter, they also offer attempts to fill me in, tough as it is to translate humor. Yet, I prefer the jokes as they tell them, "Chuck Norris drowns the sea." Or, "Chuck Norris gets in the bus and the controller pays the ticket."

The girl takes dead leaves and tosses them off the side of a cliff, one by one, while peering down. We gaze over the city, everyone glancing at my reactions, trying not to stare, trying not to ask, only to read what a visitor might see.

—Novi Sad, Serbia

Visas and Patience

He took the window seat and buckled himself in. His adult daughter shuffled belongings around the overhead compartment and gave commentary on her discomfort. He nodded at her words, not looking up or responding, but nodding so that it wouldn't seem she was talking to herself–even though she was. Remarking on how much one had to carry around all the time, and the frustrations of traveling, she stomped to the back of the plane to speak with a flight attendant before take off. In the meantime, her father made a careful study of his passport.

In the photo, he had black hair. So much had changed in the years of the passport's validity. He flipped through the visa pages, stopping to connect dates to occasions, sometimes unable to place the trip, sometimes smiling in a documented reverie. After running his fingers over one stamped visa, he began to stare at the seat in front of him, wandering into something bittersweet. His daughter huffed back to their row, slugging a glass of orange juice, and collapsed into the seat beside him, breaking into his peace. He closed his passport and slid it into his shirtfront pocket, not sharing out loud the trip he had already taken that day. He tried to look her in the eye, but she continued her ineffective list of grievances. So he clutched her free, gesturing hand and held it with kindness, with patience, until she stopped complaining, until she found she could sit still.

—Flight from Istanbul, Turkey to Budapest, Hungary

Double Date

The couple leans into the restaurant—the doorways give them plenty of clearance, but they duck down anyway. The host shows them to a table and the woman takes the chair facing the mirror. As she and her husband speak, she keeps catching glimpses of herself in the reflection just beyond him. She tries to look away, act natural, not excessively play with her smooth brown hair. Later, she holds cool eye contact with herself as she sips a glass of wine, returning to the conversation with her husband whenever he needs her. With her perfect posture, she can make out all of the angles of her face.

When the first course arrives—olives, cheese, and bread—her husband gestures for her to go first. She smiles and helps herself. She peeks in the mirror as she eats a large morsel. Suddenly, she jerks, she stops. Even fine cheekbones lose their appeal when someone chews. She coughs a bit, her husband leaning in as she grows embarrassed, covering her mouth with one hand, waving to assure him with the other. Yet, it seems there is some lesson in that bite, because she will slouch for the rest of the meal, she slumping over to keep her husband between herself and her vanity.

—Trogir, Croatia

Tram Six: Another Abbreviated Love Story

They see each other while she is a passenger and he waits at the stop. As the tram slows and the doors open, they both lift their chins just a bit. When he steps in, she looks away for a while, then they trade a half-smile over the head of the little old lady between them. The whole ride is like this—eye contact, then avoiding eye contact, eyebrows up, then eyebrows down. She glances and he notices her glance. He stares and she feels his stare. Then she studies the blank sides of buildings they pass, large inane advertisements and scaffolding. Everything outside the window seems fascinating. When she senses that he is no longer looking, she looks to him. He feels her look and aims to return it. He doesn't seem capable of becoming brave enough to speak with her. From this distance there was the potential for humiliation before so many strangers, and the older woman standing between them seems a stone fortification he can't overcome.

A few stops later, the tram slows and he slowly disembarks, feeling his lack of courage. He moves to the window by her gaze and gestures a phone to his ear. She breaks into a full smile, but shakes her head, "No."

Even if she had nodded, "Yes," the doors were quickly closing. The "Yes" would have been a horrible disappointment. It would have been a yes and a departure, a yes and a conclusion. Nonetheless, he received her smile and this is a portable success.

—Budapest, Hungary

Stealth

The little boy entertains himself with a paper airplane. People with boarding passes wait on a flight that's full-sized, but sit with quiet smiles and watch the boy's take-offs in their periphery. His paper plane falls at the feet of an airline employee and he waits for her to move. She's scanning the gate area, looking for something, looking for someone.

The boy stretches out on the floor, reaching so his hand will be at the ready. If he goes for his plane and she moves, she might spot him, or he might touch her ankle. He wishes to go unnoticed. Any of the passengers can tell that it's become quite important to him to seem invisible—his shoulders shift as he sinks into his covert mission. From his place on the floor, he can't take in the towering woman, just the height of her heel, the distance between his fingers and the wing of his lost jet. Eventually, she shifts so he can reach without giving up his position. She smiles over him, not really looking, playing the game as an unspoken agreement. She moves and he is silently vindicated as he crosses the border, recovers his aircraft, and rolls away.

Yet, his mother calls out at the last moment, startling him away from certain triumph. Probably protesting his position on the ground, she lifts him to his feet, dusts off his clothes, and moves him into her holding pattern.

—Budapest Airport, Hungary

The Rush

In Kreuzberg, in a stretch of hip shops and Indian restaurants and postcard stands, a young boy with wavy brown hair hurries down the street. In winter, the sidewalks are littered with gravel, meant to provide traction in snow. When the streets are dry, the rocks make every pedestrian unintentionally declarative, the crackling under each footstep means no one easily escapes notice. The boy cuts in and out of a line of distracted window shoppers. Tourists hear his approaching gait and clutch at their travel wallets and purses as he passes. A black Pomeranian dog and his middle-aged owner stare out of their street-level living room window, blankly watching the boy run by, not bothering to bark or growl.

Minutes later, the boy crunches a slow return, something small and clean in his hands. He wanders dreamily away from the comic book shop. He holds a new edition with reverence. The boy's pace was dilatory, joyously content, as commuters power-walking home weaved left and right to hustle around him.

—Berlin, Germany

Peripheral Vision

The old man in the shuttle explains to his wife that he's trying to put his phone on airplane mode, and he's having a heck of a time doing it. The gadget seems to confuse him, but there's also the driver who is chauffeuring us to the plane, hustling erratically around carts and trailers full of luggage. So the old man is leaning on a ledge, sometimes holding the elbow of his wife, and sometimes hoping against hope for a smooth moment as he uses both hands to deal with the phone.

He has eyebrows like Disney's Epcot shrubbery. He can feel someone studying him, but I've perfected the ability to observe someone in my peripheral vision while a point in the distance seems to hold my gaze. So when he looks over to see if I am watching him, gathering up his details —the haphazard part in his hair tended and adjusted by his wife—he believes I am merely staring out the window. He thinks I am watching the wheels of an airplane instead of his rule-abiding cell phone struggle and sweet affection for his wife. Thankfully, I can do both.

—London, England

Stories from Home: The United States of America

I'm Thinking Lovely

She parks in the first spot outside Arby's, and he waits patiently in the passenger side, readying his oxygen tank as she comes slowly around the long Buick. She wrestles with his walker, which seems to want to stay in the backseat. He makes loops with the tube between his nose and the tank, he adjusts the shoulder strap, he nods patiently as she exclaims something just before the walker comes free. She unfolds it to stay upright, soft cloth over the places where he will rest his hands, then opens his door and helps him out. A gust of wind blows her gray curls, but she secures him before patting her hair back into place. He begins his slow trek inside as she locks the door and shuts it. She peers at the car to be sure everything is in order, then takes two quick steps to catch up.

She holds the door for him these days. And as her husband moves into the restaurant, she tucks his blue dress shirt into the back of his pants. It was just a bit untucked and she couldn't help herself. He stopped and turned his head toward her slowly, as though he might chastise her for picking at him, for grooming him while he was unable to counter the maintenance. But he didn't. He leaned toward her and she leaned in as if to hear him. Then he kissed her on the cheek. She shrugged, flustered, and held open yet another door. How lovely to see in real life! How lovely to catch—at a gas station Arby's on a Sunday morning—such an enviable love.

—Exit 312, Nebraska

Fearless Zumba Septuagenarians

Zumba is a cruel trick on the elderly ladies in the sparsely populated fitness room: an eight-dollar drop-in fee for overly complicated dance steps and music featuring figures such as Pitbull, who croons words the women can't-and-likely-shouldn't comprehend. The twenty-something yoga-pant-wearing teacher encourages them to get into the songs, to shimmy and shake their chests. Our shrewd oldsters put their arms out and merely move their heads. They opt for optical illusions to preserve modesty, and not hurt the poor girl's feelings.

The enthusiastic Zumba leader stops between each song, tells them to drink water, introduces the next routine: grapevine right, tap, step out, kick, forward, back, cha-cha-cha, half step, turn, hip circle. Okay?

One meek student asks that the instructions be repeated. The teacher complies, to the continued bewilderment of the seasoned citizens, then straightens her ponytail. "Got it?"

At the cue of general shrugging, the music begins and the steps are followed with vague caution. At the end of class the teacher says, "With this last song, the woman who taught me said to walk in all sexy, like you're going into a nightclub."

One of the ladies scoffs "I haven't been in a night club in forty years." After a pause, she stands even more proudly, "Actually, fifty!"

When asked to circle their hips they just move slightly to each side. When asked to do the grapevine, they take a few paces. Yet, the long-time observers of life smile, laugh at their missteps, and wipe their brows —the joke is on Zumba. They're happy not to know.

—Colorado

The Day We Flew a Kite, Read Books, and Hid Under the Lilacs

I spent the day with my oldest niece. We flew the butterfly kite she got for Easter. Both of us kept breaking into the tune from Mary Poppins, "Let's go fly a kite…" then swiftly forgetting the rest of the words, but continuing in happy humming. The kite got stuck in a tree. I wrangled the twine while she looked up in worry. Eventually, I set the kite free, so I felt pretty darn cool.

We sat in a clearing between two lilac bushes. I told her it was my favorite place to read when I was young, so we gathered a few books and read them together. I lit up when she told me that reading is one of her favorite hobbies. We braided strands of grass for bookmarks. She yodeled at one point, "I love poetry!" I was delighted. We agreed that haiku can be tough and rhyming is awesome.

We put dandelions behind our ears—our left ears, since we're both left-handed. I love her so much, and love that we have this in common. Then back to the kite, then back to our clearing, then ice cream cones in the shade. It was the sort of day that made me wonder if we would remember it later. So just in case, here it is.

—Colorado

How to Get Rid of the Hiccups

She has the hiccups. Her husband wears a golf cap. They are extremely slow in shuffling to their Buick. The snow has turned to patches of slush, some just puddles and some quite slick. He takes her arm and they speak very quietly, but her hiccups are loud, involuntary, and they ricochet off the surrounding buildings. She mutters in her embarrassment.

They reach the passenger door and he tells her something as she lowers herself into the car. She giggles at his words, her face breaking into a gaze of love. He smiles as he closes the door, pleased that he can still make her laugh. He adjusts the cap on his head while moving carefully to the driver's side. He opens his door and she greets him with a loud HIC!

He's laughing so hard that he can't get behind the wheel, and she's volleying the laughter right back at him. Resting his arm on the top of the car, the door wide open, he tries to settle down, but they can't quite stop. As the chilly day blows around them, the parking lot echoes with a joyous older couple cracking up.

—Colorado

Prints

It's the Department of Motor Vehicles, so no one is really crossing any items off their Bucket List around here. The lack of enthusiasm shows in glum faces, distant stares, the contagious yawns. A woman in line patiently stretches. Sometimes she steps forward and raises her arms, and sometimes she leans to the side. She's making two old ladies very nervous as they wait to have their photos taken for updated licenses. This is not a place to be flexible.

A man returns to his wife, who sat in the photo-waiting area while he went up for his portrait. She greets him, "What was the fuss?"

"Oh. She said I've been working too hard."

"What's that?"

"I've got no more fingerprints–look at that. She couldn't get a read on 'em, said I've been working too hard and wore them all away."

"Well well," she moves to the door and he follows.

As he opens the door for his wife, first he takes it by the handle, then he puts his palm on the glass. He studies his palm print as she shuffles past him. She moves ahead. Trailing her, he examines his fingers, hunting for prints, looking for proof of what he may leave behind.

—Department of Motor Vehicles, Northern Colorado

Tactful (and Tattooed)

When they climb into the airport shuttle, she is in the middle of a story, her husband half-listening and half-overseeing the driver loading their suitcases. They have reached the age where drivers never allow them to move their own suitcases. She continues, "And our son, I'm sure you didn't notice, but he has two tattoos for that woman. Huge tattoos. One with her astrological sign, the other with her name. Her name."

"Well."

"And all week he's talking about the problems they are having–." She elaborates on the problems as her husband slowly notices a man across from them in the shuttle. The man has a wide assortment of tattoos on his forearm and bicep, on his neck, and one on his chest that peers out from under his t-shirt. The man tries to elbow his wife, but she keeps on talking and staring out the window.

"Ugly, huge tattoos forever! And then he tells me to be ready, because he doesn't think they have a future, but he's got her name on his arm! I thought we raised the boy to have more sense! What's he going to do? Only date women named Melody for the rest of his life?"

"You know..." The booming voice of the tattooed man across from them snaps her from her story. She studies their neighbor–his sunglasses on his head, his high-top sneakers, his decorated skin. She snaps her jaw closed in apology. "You know," the man begins again, "Your son can always just say it's his Grandma's name. If he meets someone else."

"Oh. Uh, yes, I suppose you're right," She can barely squeak out the reply, though the tattooed man smiles quite warmly.

"It works. But, yeah, I probably look like I've got a lot of Grandmas." He laughs in delight and the couple is nearly convinced to join in on the joke. Nearly, but not quite.

—Kansas City, Missouri

The Purpose of Rainboots

The little girl is hustling out of daycare with her mother right behind. It's been raining and Mom is trying to protect and preserve the handful of paper-crafts that her child produced that day. Despite the wet weather, the creations needed to get to the refrigerator for proud display. When Mom calls out, "Oh no! Don't!" I turn my head. The little girl is making a quick course to a minuscule puddle.

"Oh no," the mother notices she's drawn my attention, so she makes it clear that her scold is in jest, "Oh! Don't go into that puddle with your boots, oh no!" Mom is smiling, raising the pitch of her voice, and she glances away from her girl to give me a grin. She wants to show me that it was all in good fun, to show that the purple galoshes were selected for just this sort of day. I smile at her with admiration over so much good mothering—for preparations when there are forecasts of rain, for clutching those glue-encrusted-paper-crafts so carefully, for delighting that her daughter can truly be a child.

—Vermont

Sweet Kids: The Airplane Edition

Before we board, the mother in the pink Adidas t-shirt leaves her two daughters with her husband as she storms away to take a call, announcing to the gate area, "What? No. We couldn't find anyone to watch my kids. No one wants to do it. My kids are crazy." Nearly all the waiting passengers glance over at the father and the children, and then sadly toward their boarding passes. Some close their eyes, perhaps wishing for the young family to be in a different section during the nine-hour flight.

Naturally, it's easy to locate difficult kids on an airplane, but the excellent ones are also there. A little girl whimpers and threatens to cry as we taxi, but she's joking. In the next second she smiles and waves at her neighbors. Another child grins around his pacifier. Outside the restroom, an elderly woman rests in the jump seat. At her side is a little boy with a Curious George stuffed animal who tells passengers waiting for a vacancy, "Wait a minute! My mom is in there. I'm supposed to wait here with my monkey." People stand patiently, smiling at him, as he warns others who arrive. "My mom is in there." So pleased with his task.

And the girls previewed so poorly by their mother? They sit patiently in their seats. Their father reaches into the overhead bin to get down a favorite blanket, and they don't make a sound, other than happy-quiet laughter as they watch a movie. After all the nervous glances across the aisles, here sits hope against hope.

—Flight from Chicago to Vienna

Your Easter Dresses, Love Grandma

Grandma is buying the girls a pair of Easter dresses–the fluffier the better. Her two granddaughters stand close and grin. They love the dresses; Grandma adores the dresses. One is pink with a ruffled petticoat for skirt volume. The other dress is white with flowers and more like a bedazzled tutu. The taller of the two girls can't stop brushing her fingers against the smooth fabric while the clerk scans the tags.

Grandma delights in making the purchase, but she does slump a bit on the counter as she wrestles from her purse a shiny-covered checkbook. As she fills it out, the girls watch Grandma writing a check, like the Declaration of Independence, like she's paying in a currency as old as Grandma herself. She hands it over and there is a register of surprise from the girls when the clerk accepts this paper in exchange for their fantastic Sunday gowns. Grandma beams as the girls say in spontaneous unison, "Thank you, thank you!" And the little one hugs Grandma's legs while the older collects the dresses that have been covered in plastic to protect them from the rain. She squeezes Grandma's hand then lets her carry their winnings, the girls gazing at the ruffles as they depart.

—Colorado

New Eyes

Before the midnight flight leaves Denver, a girl at a newsstand sells me a Diet Mountain Dew for $2.55 with a straight face. There are no other customers, so she takes her time in counting the change. She disinterestedly asks, "Where are you going?"

When I tell her I am headed to Istanbul she gasps. She clutches at her heart. She is petite, suddenly so warm, suddenly so animated that her whole personality shifts. "Oh, it's been my lifelong dream to go there!" Though in her early twenties any long-held dream has still only been held for a relatively short period, this is also the time in our lives when we do still dream. So I smile even more as we visit.

Inspired by that gasp, I decide the long haul will have to be an opportunity. Even in the twenty hours of travel ahead, I pledge to consider this with a proper appreciation. So even as I climb into airplanes, even as I wait in various layovers, I will not be groggy and just wait for the time to pass. I will be open, watchful, and view this as a lifelong dream as well. I am grateful to her for a reminder that would shake me from my routines.

—Denver International Airport, Colorado

Deliberation: To Crock-Pot or Not

They were the third pair that day mulling over the used crock-pot at the back of the thrift store. A teenaged girl and her mother—the girl holding up things she thought might suit her Mother, whose eyes grew wide with disagreement. Later, the mother would suggest a sweater and watch her daughter's eyes roll. They considered the crock-pot. The daughter claimed she would definitely use it, with her friends, to, like, y'know, make some stuff. It remained unsold.

An elderly couple shuffled through, married long enough to use half the non-verbals of the mother and daughter. "Arthur?" He'd blink in her direction and she would set something down, or bring it closer for him to inspect. He sniffed toward the books and she waved him permission to skim. Later they stood over the crock-pot without a sound, staring deep into it, before they headed—empty-handed after all that browsing—toward the door.

The crock-pot received a more serious contemplation from a middle-aged woman with a silent husband. She had been giving him orders: "Look at this chair. It's nice. Sit in it." He sat. "Stand up." He stood. "Look at these shoes, do they fit?" He sat to try them. "I don't like them," she called, shaking her head. He removed them. She led him: "Look at this crock-pot." She listed the dishes her mother made in a crock-pot, and the dishes her friends had made in their crock-pots, making the whole culinary leave-it-be experience sound rather enjoyable. "I'm getting it."

Finally, the meek man spoke: "Baby. We have a crock-pot." "We do?" "We have two."

She paused for a full beat, running a mental scan of her storage spaces. "I'll have to make something in it one day." He went back to mute, nodding and following, as they moved to the register with arms overflowing.

—Colorado Springs, Colorado

Wave to Mama

A mother shuffles away from the school bus stop after her daughter has boarded. She moves like it is exceptionally early in the morning, though the sun is up and busily blinding drivers heading east. Her hair in a haggard ponytail, she pulls the sleeves of her navy sweatshirt over her hands as she moves homeward.

The girl must be one of the first picked up, as the school bus appears otherwise empty. She opens a window on the left side of the bus and extends a pink-coat-sleeved-arm, fluttering it up and down, waving to her mother's back. In the last moment, before the bus pulls away, the mother turns and sees the unanswered gesture. She awakens. She begins waving back wide, with both arms, like flagging down an airplane, then she blows her dear girl a goodbye kiss. She resumes her exhaustion only when the bus turns the corner.

—Colorado

Missing You

It's a good turnout for a morning Mass at the Irish church on the top of the hill. Though, as usual, I am the only person under 40—perhaps the only under 50. I'm accustomed to these demographics. Everyone is spread out through the center of the church. Fr. Vince has to move half-way down the aisle to give the homily. I'm delighted to smile at my fellow churchgoers when we wish each other "Peace." Few people are close enough to shake hands, so we wave across the rows. We turn forward and back, making eye contact and holding up two fingers in the V of peace, like tourists in front of a landmark.

An older man with his flannel shirt tucked into his jeans greets his neighbors and gives the peace sign off to an unaccompanied spot on his right. He nods where no one sits. He pats the empty railing next to his hand—missing someone, feeling a presence, paying tribute to one who used to sit so close. I notice how he prays with his shoulder turned slightly toward the vacant place at his side, and I really do wish him peace.

—Vermont

Happiness Granted

On a bench at the mall, a young mother rests with a baby in her lap and a toddler at her feet. She encourages the toddler, "Say Happy New Year! Say it. Say Happy New Year." The toddler is shy and leans in close.

As I pass, the boy speaks up, "Happy New Year!"

I smile over him and reply, "And Happy New Year to you!"

He glances up at me in shock, and I see for the first time the cell phone in his hand, the request cajoled for someone on the other end. "Not you!" He cries, a new frown forming on his face as he sees I have commandeered the wish, "Not you!"

His mother can't help but laugh, but she tries to correct him, "Okay, that's okay."

"No. Not you!" He calls out after me again. However, it seems he is too late.

—Colorado

The Nod

Waiting in the Arrivals Lounge, they shuffle, they pace, they gaze toward the gate area. A woman in bright white shoes tugs at the hem of her shirt in the wait, adjusts her purse on her shoulder, tugs her pockets. Another woman in flip-flops stands, rests one knee on a seat nearby and loses her shoe. She hunts for it, puts it back on, starts to bend her knee onto the seat again, stops herself only as her shoe slides off once more. It's a group of fidgeting folks, happily impatient, wearing smiles so as to be fully prepared.

A gray-haired cowboy arrives with a bouquet of flowers and his keys hanging on his hip. He sits next to me and nods, then locks his eyes toward the gates. He shifts from side to side, he glances into the flowers and takes a long, steadying breath.

White Shoes meets her adult son, fresh from a flight. She nearly cries as she holds him, a grown man with a backpack, tugging at his t-shirt like his mother. Cowboy and I both grin, first to ourselves, then vaguely toward each other. My friend exits and heads my way, she and I greet each other with big smiles and move toward the parking lot. I nod to the Cowboy once more, noticing he seems young and nervous just now. He rubs his gray beard, adjusts his hat, and nods right back.

—Colorado

Do You Hello?

Friendliness is my nature. This is such a deep instinct that I'm always the one saying hello when I pass people in public. In Vienna, when you say hello to strangers, sometimes they cross the street. In Istanbul, sometimes they follow you off the train. In Hastings, Nebraska, they say hello back. In each new place, it may be hit or miss.

Sitting in a big Chevy truck on the open roads in Kansas, I delight in the expansive skies and the tidy rows for planting. And I uncover many a mute hello. I am perched on the receiving end of acknowledgment, greetings, and well wishes from oncoming traffic. The "farm finger"—either the pointer finger or sometimes the first two fingers—raised in a quick salute to other trucks. The farmers offer a gesture of hello, sometimes accompanied by a barely visible nod of the head. My farming sources tell me the nod is for someone you know, and "the point" is for general good will.

Because here, well, we *hello*.

—Kansas

Comfort Calling

The toddler girl's hair sticks out with curls in every direction. I often notice the elderly before children, but this little girl seeks to be seen. She is sitting in the row over my shoulder and making kissing noises. I turn and she makes a fish-face at me, sucking in her cheeks. I smile at her mother, then make a similar face to the girl. We carry on, smooching at each other and giggling. Her mother passes off the girl to her father and heads to get a cup of coffee.

The toddler almost immediately begins to cry and forgets me entirely. I am no longer entertaining. She sobs for her mother, and her father tries walking her around the gate, tries pointing to the planes, the people, her toys, but she will not be mollified. Finally, he passes the last bank of payphones in the universe, and this gives her pause. He is delighted. She is satisfied to pick up the receivers as he looks expectantly away, awaiting her mother. So he doesn't notice the girl holding receivers to her ear with interest, then holding them to her mouth to taste. Instead, in his distraction, he's fine with letting her enjoy any obsolete and bacteria-laden port in the storm.

—JFK Airport, New York

The Cell Phone Slaughter of Small Talk

This was a job for the large round table in the sports bar. The Grandmother seated herself between the mother-type woman and her pretty granddaughter, whose smooth face was turned down at her purple smartphone. The girl made conversation with her Grandma from time to time, but not eye contact. A few minutes later more from the party arrived: the Dad, their high school aged son, their middle school aged son. Grandma put up her arms for a hug. The trio waved across the table and collapsed into their chairs, hurriedly checking their phones to find any news that may have been released during their laborious pedestrian commute from the car. The older brother hid under his hat and scanned facebook. The youngest boy held his phone below the table, leaning forward, trying not to be quite so blunt about his distraction. Their father set the standard and proudly displayed the many abilities of his iPhone. Grandma nodded.

The oldest daughter joined them, finally completing the group, and didn't even sit before opening her laptop. She passed this to her father who began a slideshow for Grandma of every single snapshot taken on their trip to Germany.

The kids kept to their gadgets, since we all know children should be seen and not heard. And Grandma sat politely for a while, gazing at the tops of her relatives' heads and trying to smile, before she leaned toward the mother and sighed, "Alrighty. Hon, I'm bored."

—Somewhere in Nebraska

Light Bulb in the Lighthouse

Before taking the lighthouse tour, visitors loiter at the Interpretive Center. A family with four children waits for the 1 pm tour. In the meantime, they explore the exhibits and watch a video highlighting the history of the Yaquina Head Outstanding Natural Area. The title sounds like an oversell, but it's a lovely location.

Promptly at 1, the family gathers for the tour, stands in the wind and gazes up. A tour guide in a dress and an apron steps outside to greet the afternoon group—the family with four children, a man cycling from Montana to Mexico, various couples from the Midwest, yours truly, my aunt, my sister, and my niece.

Perhaps because I am myself the fourth child, I'm smiling over the youngest from the family. She has red hair and a cascade of freckles. She listens attentively as the tour guide asks questions of the group. It's an audience participation technique, but her brothers and sister are quick to answer. She nods at the replies that her outgoing siblings supply.

Later, the guide says there will be rules for climbing the lighthouse tower: "No shouting," the redhead suggests.

The guide nods, "That's a good rule." The little girl shrugs, "You're welcome!"

The guide asks the group, "What kind of oil do you think was used to keep the lighthouse bright?"

The redhead smiles helpfully, "You know, you should really watch the video at the visitor's center."

As the guide tries to explain that she has seen it before, and that she actually does know something about the lighthouse, the assembled adults burst out in laughter, and truly begin to enjoy the tour.

—Oregon

Eye-Catching

A woman in a neon yellow button-up shirt, a white sweater, and neon yellow slacks catches the attention of a middle-aged man who suddenly can't remove his backpack properly. He gets a bit tangled up as she passes. His original idea to remove the bag and sit is lost in a flustered attempt to free himself from suddenly so many straps.

The neon lady leaves her carry-on roller bag partially in front of two vacant seats, and wanders away to talk on the phone. This catches a lot of attention as well, since unattended baggage may be destroyed, according to the robotic warning played periodically from speakers overhead. Many eyes go from the woman to the suitcase, and some passengers near the suitcase shift in their seats.

An elderly woman approaches the left-behind suitcase. She aims to move it so she can take the chair next to her husband—her rightful place, and worth touching a stranger's abandoned bag to acquire. Neon lady swoops in to wordlessly roll her bag away from the woman and in front of the fully vacant chair. She moves off to continue her phone call without a gesture of apology. The older woman huffs at the manners but accepts a tablet computer from her husband. She flips open the cover with an eyebrow up. Yet her frustration subsides quickly as she leans near her husband. He touches her arm and they huddle in and smile over photos from their newest grandchild—a brand new hope.

—Denver International Airport

Thank You for Your Service

He ambled through the aisle of the convenience store. His hat read "Veteran: World War II." I beamed at him, as I do at most elderly people, and he stopped moving so he could really smile back. He is wearing beige suspenders, navigating the store with a cane. I thanked him for his service and asked, if he didn't mind my asking, where was he deployed during the War? He was in the Pacific. I sighed. I could feel my eyebrows gathering down over my now-watery eyes. He drove a boat that took the troops to shore. He spent his 18th and 19th birthdays on invasions. He loitered by the Gatorade. I fought the urge to hug him or see if he wanted to tag along to Nebraska. Friendly has a fine line.

In the parking lot later, he labored to get into his pickup. He hoisted himself up, leaned in, leaving his cane behind, then once firmly in his seat he stretched out to grasp the handle of the cane. He placed it in the seat as a passenger. He could feel me watching him. I kept my grin wide and politely affectionate, since I didn't want him to think I was too strange. I started my car, he started his. We shared a quick departing wave of gratitude.

—Snyder, Colorado

Step Dois, Três. Turn Dois, Três

The folk dancers gather, circle out, promenade, move to the music. A man in a brown hat calls out directions, and the audience whispers, "Is that English?" The Portuguese folk dancers are performing for a mother-daughter tea party in the church basement. "No, they're speaking Portuguese." The women sit at tables with various china cups. We eat tiny sandwiches and smile politely at the entertainment.

In a white shirt with a blue sash at his waist, a gray-haired man focuses on his task of guiding the women. He is serious, glancing at the ceiling as if the next steps are printed there, or staring at the man in the hat for the next command. He is precise while the other dancers play. Naturally, he is the one I love the most, so I stop paying attention to anyone else in the rotation. How lovely to see up close the activities that people enjoy, where we invest our time, where we count our steps.

After the performance, the man slips outside for a cigarette. He gazes at the sidewalk with great concentration and mentally reviews the performance. He taps a foot forward, shifts his shoulders involuntarily. He is dancing again in muted movements, still gazing at the spot ahead of him, trying to remember if he turned left when he should have gone right.

—Colorado Springs, Colorado

The Bold and the Apprehensive

The couple boarded the plane extremely late, toting five carry-on bags between them. The flight crew looked the other way. He opened nearly every overhead compartment in their section of the plane, pacing toward the back, sneering at the more timely passengers' properly stowed belongings. He opened the compartments and his wife followed along, checking as well and slamming the overheads closed. Passengers already seated and belted pretended to stare straight ahead, but gave each other sideways glances.

He passed toward the front, opening the compartments again. His wife had given up and began forcing items under her seat. A steward tried politely to hurry the man along, asking him to sit so the flight could depart. The man flushed. He handed off one of his heavier bags like a distant relative passing a screaming child back to its parent. The steward remained patient, but made a face to his colleague and the passengers at large.

During the flight, the couple argued a bit, sighed often, stood in the aisles blocking traffic, snatched the last glasses of juice off the flight crew's service trays. When he knocked a cup of water onto his laptop and they both jumped up to dry it off, a woman to their left laughed out loud and elbowed her seatmate, demanding commiseration.

Later, during turbulence, the couple grew very anxious and sullen. She burrowed under a blanket and he held onto her, brushing her hair with his ring-fingered hand as she whimpered. And the laughing woman made a show of not being afraid, sitting up in her seat, but she also made a show of her guilt. She wrinkled her forehead, showing penitence for her prior delight in karmic justice. Blinking over at the couple, she tried tossing glances of compassion. We were all children, in the end, all afraid we might not exist.

—Flight from Frankfurt, Germany to Denver, Colorado

One Giant Leap for Ein Kleines Kind

The plastic bag is in the top of the tree. Three stories up. This distance means little to the two-foot child under the tree, leaping with his hands up, reaching and stretching for the bag. Then calling, "Get down here," as another tactic. His mother calls him in, as the afternoon is growing breezy and the bag is irreparably encased in branches far above even her maternal height.

He holds up a finger, a request for one final attempt. And with a loud tennis-player-grunt he extends, he jumps with all his energy. It's hardly a hop. An adorable one, but not quite off the ground. At a loss, he strolls sullenly back as directed. His good mother grins and welcomes him into her arms, impressed with his good will and his great attempt.

—Colorado Springs, Colorado

Learning to be Cool

The father wants to take a photograph of his daughter at the large airport window, in front of the airplane they will take to Vienna. He's removed his shoes and walks the gate area in his socks. His teen daughter lags behind him with her head bowed. She wears a pose that she hopes will distance her from the nerdy connotations of her father's rustling shoelessness. She is at the age where cool is of the essence, and equally amorphous, and perhaps frustratingly out of her reach.

The mother is as pale as a Tori Amos album cover. She observes from their set of three seats, watching over her daughter's gadgets and her husband's travel books. The daughter stands still and grumpy for the snapshot, rolling her eyes for all posterity. In the end, she won't like the process, and later she won't like the photo either. Here's hoping that one day she will blush at how dramatically she'd replied to such a slight, fatherly request. In the meantime, a few minutes after they return to their seats, the daughter ultimately reaches over and pats her father's arm–a vision of who she might become.

—Chicago O'Hare, Illinois

The Whatever Grandpa

Though there are dozens of food carts outside for the Midnight Sun Festival, she sits with Grandma and Grandpa in an air-conditioned restaurant with tall tables. She gazes at the World Cup game from time to time, or the bartender, or the waiter. Grandma is looking through photos in a digital camera, and Grandpa is on his smartphone. Their twenty-something granddaughter mumbles and Grandma advises her to, "Speak up, sweetie!"

"I'm bored," the granddaughter grows even younger as she says it, but her grandparents stick to their gadgets.

Grandpa will include her by showing off shots from an amusement park. He's pointing to a picture of himself on a ride, "They pull you down like a rubber band and let you go! You go like a rocket, up in the air, shooting up, and everything goes like–" He gestures his best impression of the slingshot movement. The granddaughter nods without really paying attention. Grandpa tries again to explain the sensation of it, how wonderful it was to take the chance, to be sent into the air! How thrilling it was, even at his age, "Especially at my age!" He's delighted, but she nods in impatience.

Grandpa turns back to his camera. "Whatever," he mutters it toward her indifference. "Whatever," he sighs the word, reliving the thrilling moment by smiling over the picture, wise beyond his years.

—Fairbanks, Alaska

Cheer Up, Buttercup

A little girl with curly blonde hair perches in her stroller with a scowl. Her mother navigates toward their departure gate, and the girl's lips are twisted, her brow gathered, her arms folded. As mother and grumpy toddler roll past a line of people waiting for a flight to Dallas, the passengers coo at the girl. She glances at the string of travelers, their faces bright, but does not blink or grin as they expect—as would be the polite response to such kind gazes. They stay optimistic as they wait. But when the girl and her frown have rolled on by, the row is crestfallen. They turn their heads, nearly in unison, to await another chance to smile.

—Denver International Airport, Colorado

Mugging

At brunch, the three young girls sit on the left of the table, and their mothers face them on the other side. The girls chat over their pancakes, modeling their mothers. The mothers laugh and sigh and give cautious looks toward their girls—checking to see if all is well, each smiling at her respective child. One of the daughters wears a purple t-shirt and is struck by a difference between her friends and their mothers. Each little girl has milk in a plastic cup with a lid and a straw. The mothers drink coffee from white mugs. She whispers conspiratorially with her pals, and they nod toward the mugs that were set on the table before anyone had arrived. Along with the knife, fork, and spoon wrapped in a white napkin, someone had already left coffee mugs at each place, expecting anyone who took a seat there to need all these dishes to enjoy their meal.

One girl beams, a second girl appears nervous, and the third charges on ahead. She slides the mug closer, turns it upright before her, uncaps her milk and pours it into the coffee mug. She wraps her hands around the porcelain; she pretends to blow at the top as her mother does. She takes a drink of her relocated milk and smiles at her friends. They also begin the sneaky process of going from plastic cups to the coffee mugs—a sign of breakfast elegance. The mothers have seen the whole process unfolding and glance knowingly at each other, delighting in the fact that their girls are still young enough to wish to be like Mom. So the six women, three taller and three shorter, become indiscernible as they chat, as they nibble, as they sip.

—Chicago, Illinois

Night Game

After dinner the small boy stood at the far side of the lawn with his back to the street. He focused on a point in front of him, waiting for the ball to come his way. He opened his mitt; he accepted what arrived, he tossed it back with full effort.

Cars slowed down as they moved past the house, predicting a runaway baseball could enter the street at any minute. He leaned left for a catch, immediately turned right for another. He seemed a dynamo from a distance, but on the approach it became clear: he had no batter, no pitcher, no partner for playing catch, and no baseball at all. A boy and a mitt alone in the lawn, living out a highlight reel with great seriousness.

His grand catch arrived. He stepped forward, back, staring up into the air. He briefly used the mitt to shield his eyes—though the sun had begun to set far to one side—and dove into the grass. He made the catch! He jumped up to celebrate with the teammates around him, sharing unmet high-fives, receiving unseen embraces and claps on the back. He called and grinned in the center of the crowd–the Team Hero was as overjoyed as they were invisible. And undefeated.

—Omaha, Nebraska

Lawn Pilot

Still only one-third of the way through his job—navigating a riding lawnmower over two acres in front of the Lutheran church—he delighted in shredding each swath. He chose a bright orange shirt that day, feeling kindred to the construction workers laboring to resurface the parallel county road. Under his floppy hat and large sunglasses, he felt vaguely invincible. The workers hammered through the shoulder, as he toppled milkweed.

Like a small child with a toy, he made airplane noises to himself. Puttering his lips, roaring like an engine, he was free to imagine aloud, unheard over the lawnmower motor and the various blasts of road restructuring. His look of amusement was visible to drivers, hands on their foreheads in the crawl through the construction zone. At nearly ten miles an hour, he seemed to fly by the idling SUVs. In sheer glee, he bounded over a large mound of grass. Now properly tended.

—Fort Collins, Colorado

The Ideal

The young mother held onto her daughter's hand as the tiny girl jumped off the curb, hustled ahead, then slowed down–her mother's arm was a satisfactory tether. The open-air shopping center had enough square footage, shops, restaurants, and parking to keep people busy as long as they wished. There were not crowds in most areas, but there was something of a congregation as the mother and child approached Victoria's Secret. The doors to the shop were propped open and a wave of perfume flooded the sidewalk. A massive photo of a furious-looking woman in underwear took up the whole window. Her hair tousled by professionals, her airbrushed body revealed, her brow furrowed with allure. The mother moved her daughter to hold her other hand, putting a barrier between child and the shop. Yet, the small girl gazed up at the advertisement, taking in this creature.

And as they passed this Ideal she pointed, in case her mother had managed to avoid the display, "Mommy, look. That girl is immodest!" Her mother nodded, relieved, and her fellow shoppers also turned their eyes away, smiling, shifting, impressed.

—Colorado

Older And Wiser (And Eating Cake!)

The treadmills hum quietly and the pair of ladies speak loudly. Their gray hair bounces, they swing their elbows. When one says, "All right, here we go," they turn up the speed just a pinch, and clasp onto the frame of the treadmill to stay upright. Moments later, one will call, "Okay! Okay!" Then Burgundy T-shirt and Teal Fleece dial back from snail-pace to iceberg-pace and resume their conversation.

They watch the long mirrored wall before them, but not to look at themselves. Burgundy admits, "I don't look in the mirror much these days. Makes me go 'Yikes!'" Teal assures her, "Yep, but we never have to pass on dessert, do we?" They tread onward with a triumphant laugh.

Teal notes that people always turn to catch a glimpse of themselves in the mirror as they walk by–young women who adjust their posture, muscular men who flex on the move. Every gym member who crosses the mirror is observed, and if their eyes seek their own reflection, our old girls giggle. "Let's just quit this and get a martini," Burgundy thinks aloud. Teal has already pushed the stop button. They head out with joy and satisfaction at a job half-done. They make panting passengers on the cardio equipment wistfully hope for their next birthday.

—Colorado Springs, Colorado

To The Happy Couple

He is one-single-year-old, toddling freely around the wedding during the toasts. He stops by a rather good audience member and distracts her. She acknowledges him politely, seeks for his parents, shifts under his stare. His brown eyes stay locked on her face. He wears a button-up shirt, boots, a brown fauxhawk. When she reaches her hand down to him, he gasps her finger. He holds it tight and stands very still.

She murmurs to him while others offer congratulations on the microphone. She smiles. He gazes without a sound. She is of the age where people feel pity if you seem to enjoy children, but don't yet have children. In this vein, she pushes her lips into a more subdued smile. She tries to temper her delight. She peers around to see if anyone else sees what sees–this silent little angel who holds her in his sights.

—Colorado Springs, Colorado

Health and Wellness

The old man winks at a woman on a stationary bike, the kind where one can sit upright with the pedals before them. He is pushing seventy, or pulling eighty. He follows the directions of a twenty-something trainer toting a yoga ball. Our senior does vague squats, slight lunges, and ends with his back to the wall as though sitting in an invisible chair. Low reps. He keeps glancing at the woman on the bike.

Her hair is gray and pulled into a bun at the top of her head. She gazes at the televisions above her. One set features a cooking program that she has more than once scoffed over, making hand gestures of disbelief. After the sly man's session is done, he passes her one more time, smiling in her direction. He goes to the lockers and returns with a portable oxygen machine. Not just any oxygen machine—but hers. He helps her to stand; he gives her some of his water. She fills him in on the unbelievably decadent cooking show. They wipe sweat from their foreheads discreetly before he leads her slowly and supportively to their car.

—Colorado

Crabby and Flirty

"I've been here 26 years," a crab catcher tells the woman in the bulky navy coat. She'd been sitting in her car, watching the crabbing, perhaps waiting on one of the yellow-rain-coated men on the dock. A minute ago she exited to have a cigarette and take in the fresh air. This man advanced upon her like the flapping seagulls when the crab traps were raised. "I like those spots over there. I think it's deeper on that side of the dock." He wears his wallet on a chain, and paint and seawater dapple his gray sweatshirt. He keeps his brown hair long, coiling rather neatly from under his blue baseball cap. He approached the woman on her right, so she saw his left profile in her periphery when they stared over the water. From that angle, she couldn't see the giant neck tattoo on his right side.

He smokes and chats with her. She tucks her brown scarf around her neck as the wind gusts her cigarette ashes away. He extends his hand, and she pushes up her glasses before accepting his handshake. "I'll be out there on Saturday and, no, Saturday and Monday, in the morning. Sunday I'll be busy." He outlines his social calendar and she nods.

When she turns to laugh at something he's said, her age becomes clear. She is older than him by at least decade, perhaps two, and flattered and shy. "Nice meetin' you," he calls as he departs.

"You too, Mark..." She flips her feathered hair over her shoulder and takes a grinning gasp at the sea.

—Waldport, Oregon

Double Czech

The Czech woman forgot her hearing aids. She is supposed to be doing the Reading at Mass, but there are two options in the Lectionary and, "Oh dear, oh my, I do not know which I must read..." She polls a woman in the neighboring pew, but her question comes with such unintentional volume that the whole chapel becomes privy to her dilemma. She hustles to the podium to investigate the two options. She confers with a woman in the front row, who recommends that she ask the Deacon. She tracks the Deacon, who seems to be saying "The First." She hears, or chooses to hear, "The Second, okay, the Second."

He tries to correct her as she rushes away. Agreeing with his unheard suggestion, she relays the already broadcast message to the friend in the front, then her neighbor near the back. The crisis has been averted—without anyone noticing, she beams. "Yes, I will read the Second one."

Then she offers one more non-clandestine stage-whisper to her neighbor, just before the shaky *a cappella* hymn begins, "Good, yes. The First reading is a little fluffy anyway."

—Colorado Springs, Colorado

Stay Fickle

Gazing at each other through their thick glasses, smoothing their sweaters, two little old ladies were at an age not to care, but still cared, vaguely—mostly about what they thought of each other. As they waited for their flight, seated near the gate and assessing their fellow passengers, they arranged their handbags securely in their laps. It became a habit to feel one could be mugged at any moment.

The woman with larger glasses and a floral-print embroidered purse shrugged like a teenager as she bragged: "I used to walk six miles a week."

"That's so good for you." The second woman nodded and touched her hair, not fully gray like her companion, still honey-colored in places. "Walking is very good for you."

"Yes, but now *he* drives me everywhere."

A blink, an elevation of volume, "Oh. That's nice."

"Yes, but I've put on weight."

"Oh dear." A blink, the suppression of a smile, "That's not good."

—JFK Airport, New York

Concerto for Cello and Springs

An infant boy in red-footed-pajamas races down the moving sidewalk. His curly locks bounce as he bounds. Bystanders cringe as he nears the end, his father breaking into a sprint to swoop him up or console him quickly, depending on the outcome. But the boy prances upright off the sidewalk and rushes on past the newsstand, sliding on the bottoms of his socks. He glides happily along on the slick stone floor—the moving sidewalk a race, and this the ice skating portion of his wait for the family flight.

He skates past a man in a black bowler hat playing a cello. The boy's laugh lulls people more effectively than the centuries-old serenade. The man with the cello keeps his head down, tries closing his eyes to play, but the roaming boy, the growing laughter keeps the cellist peeking from under his brim at the case full of change on the floor at his feet.

—Portland, Oregon

Driving Questions

It's hard to hear their actual conversation. There's the kind, booming voice of the bus driver, the questioning tone of the young, blonde boy. The boy wears a Transformers t-shirt, and it's his first time on a bus. His father sits nearby while the boy asks the driver about the new bus lane, about the passengers, about whether he likes driving people from place to place. The bus driver tells him fascinating facts about the newly minted bus system in town. Of particular interest to the boy are the mirrors he uses to watch the doors on the back, to be sure people get in safely and to close them when everyone is inside.

At a stop, as a family boards near the rear, the boy hops to try and get the same view as the driver. The driver explains, then asks the boy to check his work. The boy turns to confirm that the family is already seated, then he gives the driver an all-clear. The boy studies the features of the bus, and the driver warmly replies to the ceaseless questions. In fact, the passengers can see—from their view of the driver's eyes in the now-infamous mirror—how the driver smiles, how the driver is delighted to be interviewed.

—Colorado

Peace: Or the Days You Could Fit Your Knees Into Your Shirt

They're early for Mass—the Dad and his young son. The boy totes a plush Luigi from Super Mario Brothers. He wears black and neon yellow shoes that light up when he walks. When they stop at the pew, the boy kneels in a perfect genuflect, following his Dad's example.

During the readings, he is less engaged. He sits with his knees up to his chin, tugs his red shirt down over his knees. He boxes himself in, pulling his arms in from his sleeves, and smiling up at his father. His father smiles back, then feels a wave of pressure that perhaps he should be exhibiting some discipline. He scans the neighboring old ladies—all grinning at the boy who has turned his t-shirt into a home. The dimple in his pre-school cheek would get him anywhere.

Later he frees himself, jumps up as the Our Father approaches. He delights in holding his Dad's hand and mouthing the words he's not too sure of yet. After the prayer, he knows it is time to shake hands with the adults around him, to say, "Peace Be With You." His Dad nods toward an incredibly tall elderly man on their right. The tiny boy balances himself to take a few steps across the kneeler, cranes his neck all the way back and all the way up, and raises his tiny arm for a handshake. The man cranes himself down to wish the boy peace. As he lumbers back to his Luigi, to his place beside his father, blinking lights down the aisle, the boy seems peaceful indeed.

—Colorado

Respect Your Elders

Pantera is the name of a heavy metal band from Texas, and this name is scrawled across his t-shirt. He gruffly approaches the Information Desk, and his girlfriend stands at his side. The Pantera supporter begins sweetly requesting something from the antique lady sitting at the Booth. She has a binder and a telephone. His girlfriend has a smartphone, a cheetah-print backpack, and an impatient look on her face. Yet, the young man has his attention focused on the elderly assistant while she hunts for an answer. She can't seem to find what she's seeking in the printed pages before her. She lifts the telephone receiver very, very slowly. The girlfriend begins to search on her phone as well. Perhaps it is a sort of race, but it's clear that Pantera is rooting for the oldster. There's a long pause before the girlfriend is about to speak, but the Info Lady interrupts to point them in the right direction.

Pantera lights up completely when the lady wins—when paper and a telephone beats the Internet. His face rises, he shrugs sideways, he pulls in his arms. He looks like he must have when he was a child, when small things delighted him, when he didn't listen to metal music and walk with an obligatory strut. He smiles at the Info Lady, thanking her with a grin. As he turns away, he keeps the expression, basking in the way things used to be.

—Chicago, Illinois

Icy Conditions

In the middle of Pennsylvania, after driving through sleet and ice for five hours, it is a relief to take a break and smile at the two older men sitting for coffee at the gas station. I offer a delirious grin in their direction.

I ask the clerk about the remarkable church on the hill just above us. "St. Basil, I think," she shrugs as though she'd barely noticed it. The whole time I fueled up my car, I kept staring over my roof rack at the steeple. Perhaps I noticed the church because of the prayers I'd been practicing in gratitude for windshield wipers, GPS, and hearty tires. However, I'd also like to hope I am feeling more attuned to all of my surroundings. I often worry that when I come home to the United States, I'll get into the rhythm of home and forget to pocket these small moments. So I'm collecting them carefully.

The little old men are at two different tables, but they face each other. So from time to time they call out a comment, but I don't have time to commit to a conversation. I tell them Happy New Year, head to my car, remember the receipt didn't print at the pump, and smile sheepishly at them as I wipe my shoes again to approach the counter. I smile once more at my departure, "See you in a minute," one man calls, and they both chuckle. I blush and shrug in acknowledgment, as all those nerves from the slick roads and slow-going fade away in their echoing laughter.

—Somewhere in Pennsylvania

Paige M.J. Erickson

Black and Gray

His set is winding down, but the guy with the guitar has a few more songs in him. The women who were singing along with his 90s rock covers have already headed home. There are a few other patrons, most watching basketball, so he plays a few songs he's been meaning to practice. A couple enters and moves to the bar. The man has a scattering of hair remaining, and the woman has a mane of gray that she touches like a teenage girl. They are smiling and laughing, they leave their coats, and he leads her to a semi-abandoned part of the sports bar. Near the musician, there is just enough room to dance. The guitar player is plucking a medium-tempo version of Pearl Jam's "Black," which isn't exactly apt for a tango, but the music doesn't matter. They are happy to spin out, to return, to put their arms around each other. She is happy to have him lead.

I am watching them like it is a dance recital full of my loved ones. I can't break my gaze, even when my friend tries to tell me something. Instead, I wonder about their story–have they been married long? Have they just met? Are they always like this? And they never notice anyone watching, which is part of what makes this scene so lovely. They aren't dancing to be seen, they are dancing to be free.

—Vermont

In the Fridge

Of course, I'm chatting with the driver of the shuttle from the parking lot to the Boston airport terminals. The minute I walked up to the bus he said, "Look at you, so happy!" After this sort of greeting, I can't just turn back to my text messages. Instead, he tells me about his first winter in Boston. He's originally from Ethiopia, and though this winter has been rough, he said the worst was his first.

When he arrived in America, his cousin came to greet him, bearing a coat and several layers. When they left this very airport for the parking lot, my driver asked, "Are we in a basement?" Back home the only cold level in a house was the basement. There was no heating or air conditioning back home. It was important to him that he firmly established the contrasts with "back home," but he did so with glee and good timing.

So later that day at his cousin's house, he began to feel warmer, not realizing the home had been heated. He believed he had just magically acclimated to the cold or that it wasn't so cold after all. When they planned to go out in the afternoon, he saw the sun in the sky and insisted he wouldn't need any winter gear.

His cousin opened the refrigerator and indicated the light bulb that illuminated the space. "This bulb is like that sunshine outside. It does not make things warm." The driver stayed firm until they opened the door to the house, the burst of frigid air chased them back, and his cousin moved slowly, slowly, slowly while getting things ready to leave. So my driver had a convenient chance to change his mind, to bundle up, without losing face. As he puts himself back into the scene, he shivers even now and laughs—delighted to tell his story of firsts.

—Boston Airport

Camouflage

It's a chilly morning. All the kids waiting on school buses are wearing coats, but many are also wearing shorts. By afternoon it will be warm, yet there are shivers right after breakfast. For blocks you can see the bundles—a parent and their child, a kiddo and a backpack, a bus slow and yellow.

A father waits with his elementary-aged son. Dad rocks from his heels to his toes. The boy zips up his leaf-mottled camouflage jacket and wants to show off its qualities. He puts the hood over his head and dashes near some shrubs. The boy freezes, one arm up and the other down like someone paused a sprinter mid-step. The boy stands still, but he's also shaking in restrained giggles. The father pretends his son can't be seen, leaning this way, then leaning the other, putting his hand above his eyes and calling out, "The bus is coming! Where are you?"

The boy laughs aloud and emerges from the foliage. His father moves in exaggeration to demonstrate his surprise. They hug hard when reunited, and then the boy's ride arrives. As the bus rolls away with his son onboard, the father shakes his head. He is still smirking as he sets off for home. He takes a red leaf from one of the nearby bushes, and he tears it while he goes.

—Colorado

My Journey Home

TSA security at O'Hare Airport is making me cry. I receive glares, short-tempered orders, eye rolls, and blank stares. After twenty hours of travel, I have tears in my eyes during my pat-down. I realize that no one I've dealt with at security has seen me as a human being, including the woman with her hand inside the waistband of my pants.

At my gate, a huge, strong man from Chicago asks if I'm okay. I try to keep the details to a minimum so I can aim to let it go, and he shakes his head. "How could they be mean to you? If I were there, I would have told them to leave you alone."

"Then you may not have made it through," I smile and sniffle.

"My flight's delayed, girl. I've got time."

His name is Antoine. He works with concrete on overpasses in Fort Worth. He's come to town to see family and look after his mother. We talk about heat tolerance, Peyton Manning, and going to the gym. He works ten-hour days and comes home exhausted, but he said he still has to lift weights so he can have more energy. Strong work ethic is one of my favorite human qualities—right up there with compassion.

Then in line for my flight, I am greeted with a huge, warm smile from a young man who just joined the US National Guard, just as his father and grandfather had. Cody is kind, authentic, and happy. We become fast friends and fill the jetway with our laughter.

Cody and Antoine are the best of America. They welcome me home. They step in to help me smile through the frustrations of the last leg. As I sit in the plane, I realize how similar these encounters are with the people I've met on my journeys. So while one may always encounter the day-spoilers, here's to the day-savers.

—Home. USA

Dogs and Cats (Well, Just One Cat Story)

Packs of Blondes

Granted, it was a small sample, but from the Turkish TV dramas I'd watched in passive attempts to learn the language, all of the blonde women were evil. One Turkish mother called me Caroline, which I interpreted as a sort of odd pop culture compliment, until I learned that in this particular series, Caroline was a German vixen who stole a Turkish man from his wife and five children. Later in the show, the wife met Caroline in the street and stabbed her. I briefly considered life as a brunette.

One afternoon, I stopped at Taksim Square to sit, take notes, attempt to collect the pieces of that day. A blonde stray dog spotted me, circled me, and rested nearby. I tried various English and Turkish words to encourage him into depart–to no avail. He only came closer and made himself at home against my boot.

Tourists paused from placing their children in circles of pigeons while armed with cups of birdseed. Instead, they snapped pictures of the resting blondes. I tried to look faraway and at ease, mimicking the dog. I remembered why this moment felt familiar. My new Turkish companion resembled a dog I'd met before.

Two years prior, I went through Tivat, Montenegro. It was hard to sleep when serving as a feast for mosquitoes, so I embraced an early morning and fled my unsavory hostel for a walk near the water. I reached the boardwalk and watched an old man go to the edge, take off his shirt and shoes, and leap into the sea.

A blonde stray dog crossed my path. I tried to ignore him, but he was also coy and let me lead. I stopped at a bench, staring over the water, reminding myself to savor the morning and all of its details. The new friend hung out as well, just passing the time in my vicinity.

A pack of six or seven massive strays came rushing down the waterfront. They were largely menacing in their number, their speed, and in the fact that other than the man in the sea, I was completely alone.

I briefly lamented my childhood pets–outdoor cats, a bunny, a retired pony. Maybe people raised with pups wouldn't have panicked the approaching dogmob. Yet, the blonde one who adopted me stood, sniffed, marched a few paces away, and barked. He barked not with ferocity, but with an apparent sort of doggish authority.

The other pack grew attentive. They stopped short and waited. When Ol' Blondie held firm, they turned together and rushed in the opposite direction. My dog returned, marching around me with pride and coming to rest at my feet. I shared the meat from my sandwich and promised that, along with the details of the morning, I would not forget him. Here's to the beauty of being protected.

—Istanbul, Turkey

Relieved

A stray dog prowls the rather vacant beach. Lean and leisurely, he weaves around people sunning themselves like he's a bored security guard. He heads for an unattended pile of belongings. He wanders up to the beverages, discarded clothes, and sunglasses. Humans recently vacated this area. Humans left these garments behind so they could step into the sea. He sniffs at the brightly-colored beach towel, admiring it for a moment. Then, of course, he lifts his leg and pees on it.

A woman standing in the water raises her hand to her forehead to shield her eyes from the sun. She squints to get a better look. Is that a dog by her family's things? The bold beast kicks dirt over the area he claimed, to prove he was there, to prove he paid a visit while they were elsewhere. He sniffs once more and dances away as a lady in the water waves at his departure.

—Kuşadası, Turkey

The Beloved

It's an ordinary stoplight. Everyone is waiting for permission to move on. The blonde dog shivers, always nervous to ride in the car, even after an adventurous walk through the English Garden. The dog blinks his long eyelashes and pants as his owners pet him, encourage him to be brave. A small girl in the backseat of a neighboring car spots the dog. She crawls up to stand in the lap of her mother, nearer to the window, nearer to this fascinating creature. The girl has perfect dark curls, and the dog luminous blonde fur. The girl leans against the window as the hands of her mother hold her steady, smiling at this act of independent curiosity. The girl never breaks her gaze from the dog, her smile beaming through the tinted glass. The dog never notices the girl, though his owners do. They wave, the small hand now waving back, as both cars roar away, parting the much-admired pair.

—Munich, Germany

You're a Stray and That's Okay

The woman proudly marches with a designer purse and sunglasses, but she also totes a plastic bag of cat food. She stops along the sidewalk to give a handful of tiny brown squares to one of the many stray cats of Istanbul. She crouches low to the ground, her expensive belt showing, and murmurs to the kitty. People at a nearby bus stop are watching with a sort of fascination. Old men loiter to take in the scene. A girl points, causing her mother to look toward the fancy feast.

The woman has carried cat food along, so she was clearly hoping for a feline encounter. It seems remarkable to have a glamorous woman pause and chat with a cat in the middle of the day. After sufficient cuddles and coos, the woman stands. By reflex, she straightens her clothes. Her hair has fallen over her face, so she runs a cat-food-covered hand through her long locks before realizing what she's doing. She stops and stares at her hand, the hand that feeds, before hunting for a tissue in her likely-full-of-calico designer purse.

—Istanbul, Turkey

Someone to Watch Over Me

The lady behind me at the stoplight has a very tired looking Guardian Angel figurine hanging from her rearview mirror. For good reason. Since pausing, she's been engaging in an animated discussion with her Miniature Pinscher, in a smashing red-doggy-turtleneck. She sets her pup on the steering wheel. She wanted him to have a better view of the intersection. He tolerated her rather well. It took an eternity for the light to change, and she seemed distressed by the wait. To entertain him, of course, she took the opportunity to memorialize their Valentine's Day drive. She cuddled up by the dog, pouting out her lips in affection, and snapping some candid shots on her phone. When the light turned green, he slid below the dashboard, back into her arms, knowing he was loved.

—Colorado Springs, Colorado

Bitte Schön

He stands up when the little old lady comes through the doors to offer his seat to the woman. It is mid-day in the U-Bahn, not a rush hour, but so many are sitting with newspapers covering their faces, like shy movie extras. The non-descript Austrian businessman sets himself apart by his politeness.

However, the old woman doesn't see him rise, doesn't notice him clearing a place, as she is deep in discussion with her pint-sized dog.

Because she doesn't take the place he offers, he is torn between getting her attention, and re-taking his seat. He keeps jostling two teenage girls with overly thin eyebrows that lift then drop with annoyance as they hold their ground. His knees bend like Charlie Chaplin, but he hovers above the seat, then stands again. This tall man tries to take up no space, tries to go back to being part of the crowd as he reddens and shifts.

Finally, the woman seems to be looking toward him, her head tilting up from her sole companion, but she is only in a trance, staring past the offered seat and his act of kindness.

At the next stop, the misguidedly chivalrous man of the U-Bahn exhales. He opts to exit in an embarrassed rush. And he pushes through the unmoving passengers, jostling the old woman who tsk-tsks to her dog before she notices a vacant seat.

—Vienna, Austria

Must Love (Beware of) Dogs

It's a damp Sunday morning. There's a vague rain and a gray haze. Between the center of the city and the airport, patches of trees are a deep green like I've seen in the Pacific Northwest. Taxis and buses rush through, relocating puddles onto pedestrians. Graffiti covers every flat surface and a few corners as well. It's early enough that a few people are dashing to make the train, and a handful hustle to church, but mostly the humans are scarce.

An old woman with a headband is feeding snacks to a dog outside a closed car-repair shop. She stands under a "Beware of Dog" sign with a smile. She tosses nibbles between barbed wire and the fence as she chats with her four-legged acquaintance. She's leaning in with joy. For a guard dog, he lays his guard down, happy to be tamed with treats.

—Budapest, Hungary

Crossing Guard

I'm waiting to cross the street, watching for a few hustling taxis to pass, when I feel a presence on my right. I instinctively move a bit to my left. I am polite, and I know that when I am on one side of a street, people have a tendency to want to stand in front of me. Though I generally overtake them within about three or four paces, there's something about my paused self that must appear—falsely— like a slow walker.

As the final taxi zooms by and the coast is clear, I notice that the figure on my right is a stray dog. The dog has been waiting with me for a clearing, and when I begin to move, he crosses at my side. I feel delighted that I have led him to a safe retreat. It seems an honor that one of the city's stray dogs would trust my judgment.

Then I notice a few more dogs crossing. It seems that rather than leading, I am a part of a herd materializing from behind several parked cars. At the next crossing, one brown dog cuts ahead of me. Another mutt jogs, turning his head to see if I am coming along. I'm laughing aloud at my quick demotion from shepherdess to sheep. I hear more laughter and notice a group of older women observing my encounter and enjoying it immensely. I smile in their direction, happy to be accepted, as my pack runs on without me.

—Izmir, Turkey

On Dogs and Tough Guys

The slim, green-eyed teenage boy wears the now-typical skinny jeans, flashy shoes, and black puffy coat. He stands with his elbows out a bit, holds his arms away from his frame, pretending he takes up more space. When larger boys board, he stretches even taller. He shifts his jaw and flares his nostrils while nodding to the music on his headphones.

Then a woman boards with a dog. He is cracked from his serious glare when he spots the red puppy. The façade falls as he makes small, playful faces at the little creature. The boy smiles to himself as well. And the dog stares back with rapt attention toward what he so easily brought down to earth.

—Vienna, Austria

ACKNOWLEDGMENTS

Thank you to my family and friends who have been supportive of this project for many years. I am grateful to my blog subscribers for reading and sharing, following along, and leaving your comments.

Thank you to my dear family who had to endure storing my belongings, getting all of my mail, and worrying about my whereabouts for several years. I am so fortunate to have you in my life.

Much love to those who have been with the blog for the long haul: Nora Sasvari, Matthias Hilse, Gonzalo Torres, Jan Kolafa, Rich Lloyd, Amber Suhr, Ellen Liebl, Christina van Ittersum, Steven Lincoln, Clayton Lovett, Alexander Raggio, and Karma Chavez.

Thank you for inspiring me to get started, Manda Bartlett, and for help with edits and adjustments. Thank you to the talented Hüseyin Artuk for the cover design.

I'm delighted to have readers like Vintageport, Sweetexp, Kitten, and Pamela Rice. I've gotten to know fellow bloggers along the way and I am so grateful to this community—Jeff Walker, M-R Stringer, Darlene Foster, and Jo-Anne Meadows.

I am grateful to Mitch and Louann Rohse for passing on the blog to their friends. Aunt Louann, I wouldn't have put this together if it weren't for your recent pep talks. Thank you!

All my best,

Paige